Poems from the Gravel Road

poems by

Sarah Voss

Finishing Line Press
Georgetown, Kentucky

Poems
from the
Gravel Road

Copyright © 2022 by Sarah Voss
ISBN 978-1-64662-820-9 First Edition
All rights reserved under International and Pan-American Copyright Conventions. No part of this book may be reproduced in any manner whatsoever without written permission from the publisher, except in the case of brief quotations embodied in critical articles and reviews.

Publisher: Leah Huete de Maines
Editor: Christen Kincaid
Cover and Interior Art: Sonna Voss
Author Photo: Matt Goodlett
Cover Design: Sonna Voss

Order online: www.finishinglinepress.com
also available on amazon.com

Author inquiries and mail orders:
Finishing Line Press
P. O. Box 1626
Georgetown, Kentucky 40324
U. S. A.

Table of Contents

Prologue: The World Keeps Shifting

A Short History of Grandmothering

    May Day 3
    What My Young Granddaughter Should Know 4
    The Day Johnny Bit His Dad 5
    Options 6
    After Seeing Pricey Works of Art in the Local Gallery 7
    Thirteen 8
    Sixty-nine 9
    The Old-Fashioned Treasure Hunt 10
    Taking Grandson to His Piano Lesson 12
    Thanksgiving Pome 2019 14
    Fifteen 15
    Requests 16
    How to Have Real Fun and Enjoy It Too, In Hindsight 17
    Great-Grandmother's Legacy 18
    Hard Decisions 19

Like a Polaroid Picture Developing While I Watched

    Marbles 23
    Lullaby 24
    For Rob on Father's Day 25
    The In-Laws Help 26
    My In-Laws Help Again 27
    Named for Both Sides of the Family 28
    Perfume 29
    Just Once in My Life 30
    Going to Mother's on Her Eightieth Birthday 32
    Grieving 34
    One Day I Came Home and Heard a Man in My House 35
    When the Last Child Leaves Home 36
    The Old Dollhouse 37
    Graduation Song 38
    Reflections on Doing Nothing (*for Sonna*) 40
    Blessings from the Bride's Mother (*for Sonna and Chris*) 41

    A Found Poem 42
    How to Make a Mean Cat Like You ("Enhanced" Version) 43
    My First Husband Visits after Twenty Years 44
    Sestina 46
    Velvet Costumes and the Period Art Project 48
    Portrait by an Unknown Girl 49
    My Son Sent Flowers 50
    Prime Rib 51
    New Sheets on My Daughter's 50th Birthday 52

The Past Revisited Is a Door Ajar
    August in Austinburg 57
    Smelt 58
    Farm Fugue 60
    Three Silos 61
    Things Daddy Would Never Tolerate 62
    Still Standing There 63
    My Mother's First Home 64
    The Cost of a Medium-Sized Dog 67
    Not Everyone Can Ride a Bike 68
    Patience 69
    Picnic at Thompson Ledge 70
    Another View of Those Maples 71
    Stained Glass 72
    After 73
    The Gravel Road (by the Omaha Home) 74

To Ride the Wheels of Change Sweetly
    Stones Last 77
    Old, Full Baskets 78
    Forty 79
    Grandma's White Horses 80
    The Church, the Stone, and the Grass Widow 82
    Songs of Tomorrow 83
    Metamarriage 84
    Violets 85
    Umbrella Dance in Chocolate Time 86
    Exactly 87
    Second Chance 88
    World Without Complaint 89
    Two Days Before Thanksgiving 90

Love 91
And None of Us Young Anymore 92
About Family on this Road Traveled 94
My Mixed Sermon: Short, but No Jokes 96
Sister 97
Birthday Reunion 98
Lost Words 99

Conversations with My Ninety-Year-Old Mother

A Questionable Move 103
Chairs with Wheels 104
Smiling Over Her Hot Fudge Sundae 106
Mother Laughed When She Read *Smiling Over Her Hot Fudge Sundae* 107
According to Mother (When Asked) 108
Mother's Good vs. Bad Days, According to Me 109
Mother's Men 112
As Her Sixty-Something Son-In-Law Leaves, Mother Says to Him 113
Doctor Visits 114
Mother's Mother (In Her Words) 115
Breaking the Rules 116
Watson and Mother 118
Mother Is Right 120
My Life Goes Back 121
Learning New Things 122
Things I Want To Say About Being Ninety 124
Mother Wrote It Herself 125
Lamentations 126
Little by Little We Slip 128
Just Miniscule Clots in the Arteries of Daily Living 130

Fifth Seasoner

Einstein Missed the Point 133
On Being a Woman of a Certain Age 134
At the Front Window 135
Have You Reached the Part about the Lightning? 136
My Husband the Genius 137
The Christmas We Bought Each Other Hearing Aids 138
When I Am Alone 139
Sabbathing 140

Holy, Holy, Holy 141
The Weed that Turned into a Zinnia 142
Wave At Each Other 143
Memory Pill 144
Sometimes, When the Flowers Need Watering 145
Untitled 146
Sisters-by-Law 147
On the Eve of a Hard Seventy 148
Bouncing Boxes 150
The Seasons of our Emotions 151
In My Garden 152
Waiting for the Number 153
We Were Going to Have a Party 156

Acknowledgements **157**

About the Author **161**

For Family—past, present, and future.

With special gratitude to Sonna, who originally suggested I put together this collection of poems ("It will be like a little family history, Mom.") and who then helped me with it in every way possible.

And with extra appreciation to my youngest daughter Melinda, who listened to every complaint, worry, and dream I had about the process and always offered encouragement and wisdom.

And with thanks to my son Wil for his bottomless tech support.

And to my spouse Dan Sullivan, for his endless patience and loving care.

Prologue: The World Keeps Shifting

It's a task to keep up, says my friend
in his email letter sent maybe an hour ago
from some city on the other side of the globe.
For a moment I think of another friend
who's convinced that Alzheimer's results
from sensory overload. Sometimes I just
want to crawl into a poem and sleep forever.

May Day

Cold rain with snow predicted. Yesterday—
the last of a week of glorious sun—I planted
baby annuals. Today I rush to cover
their vulnerability with old sheets, wrap
three hanging baskets in terrycloth, close
the soft material with red plastic
clothespins I found in this, my new
old home, the downsizing nearly complete.

I remember being a little short of seven
and filling homemade paper baskets with candy,
wild violets and John-Deere-yellow dandelions.
Mother drove me from the farm into town
where I selectively placed my precious
gifts by various doorways, ever quick to run
away before my identity was discovered.

I raised my children in seven different houses.
Nobody marked May Day this way in the first
six, but in the seventh, the one that lasted
thirty years, the doorbell rang on May 1st.
We found cups with popcorn, candy, and a few
store-bought posies by our front steps. Some
rituals don't die, they simply commute.

This is my eighth house since my first child
arrived. Now seven decades in and the grandma
of five, I sit fearless in a tiny room I claim
as my new office, look out the window at my new
old trees scarcely swaying in the still-mild wind.
A storm promises worse tomorrow, but I am
unafraid of this coming change because over time
I've discovered that new flowers always overflow
my cup with reliability and surprise.

What My Young Granddaughter Should Know

Enrapt, Raya watches the four
music-makers, just four foreign
men intent on their work.

Her three-year-old body
already twitches in time
to the drummer's bewitched beat, heat

rising everywhere

flooding the room

my grandmother's heart
old worn passion-regulator
not yet drained, desire

still startling my imagination
those four beautiful Latinos
so ripe, so unforgettably ready.

The Day Johnny Bit His Dad

was the last day in the old house.
They were eating lunch, brought in,
all six circled 'round the table, boxes
everywhere, kitchen cabinets bared,
toys packed in plastic bins, the dog
nervous and the cat critical. Johnny's

older sisters, six and four, sandwiched
Grandma, who was staying "longer
than anyone had ever stayed before."
Johnny's mother (her belly a big ball,
everyone hoping she didn't go
for at least a couple more days)

was simply glad to be sitting down,
even the stairs making her breathless,
and Johnny's dad (just back from
his morning trip to the new house,
twenty minutes away and twice
as much footage) catching his own

breath, not enough sleep but
really everything going smoothly,
considering, and grace just sung, *the Lord*
is good to me, and so I thank the Lord
for giving me the things I need,
the sun and the rain and the apple seed ...

then Johnny slipping from his chair, doing
what any two year-old red-headed kid might
when the world turns upside down,
not understanding why Dad, red-faced,
suddenly roared, Dad's surprise a volcano
shocking the room as greatly as his speedy

exit, the teeth having drawn real blood.

Options

Today is sore from all the emotion it's carried.

Six wakes at 3 a.m. crying. Her ear aches. She
wants Mommy. Daddy can't find the chewable
pills, substitutes infant aspirin (unpacked).

Four consumes two pouches of oatmeal
(colored dinosaur eggs hidden in the flakes),
a bowl of frosted mini wheats ("Empty
the milk out first, Gramma!"), then Cheerios.

Two doesn't want to eat breakfast, get dressed,
go to the sitter, but does all three and more.

Gramma locates the right pills, drives Six
to her new school, sits in a chair too small,
admires Teacher's skill, wonders why some
teachers are natural while others aren't.

Mommy brings Baby home from the hospital,
her forty-eight hours up at 2 a.m. though it's 2 p.m.
before she actually arrives at the new front door,
the red paint job so poor they'll surely complain.

Dad adjusts the water pressure in the just-built
house; a mountain of chores sits on his shoulders.

The dog, mother, first- and last-born children
lounge on the queen bed in the plush master suite
while Dad picks up the others from daycare,
twenty-five minutes away near the old house.

Gramma rests, recalls days long gone, wonders
should she start supper, stop taking her heart
medicine, let nature follow its own course, how
she can be sad, mad, glad, scared all at once.

After Seeing Pricey Works of Art in the Local Gallery

my nine-year-old granddaughter and I
make our own. *Bloom* emerges
from a round cardboard tube meant
for mailing rolled papers. We coil
ropes, wires, and yarn around it,
then cover the upper third with rags
torn from flowered fabric found
in the sewing drawer. An antique
oriental mirror fits the lid perfectly,
reflects a circular perversion
of an ancient Chinese curse: may
your life bloom in interesting ways.

Half Done, a similar effort, begins
months later, after she leaves. I spray
a junked umbrella-stand black, wrap it
to the middle with rope recycled
from a previous existence as the edge
of a border high on my library wall.
Such patience it took to braid one-
hundred-sixty linear feet of yellow,
red, purple, brown yarn, then, when
repainting the walls, I yanked it off,
how it lay for days coiled like a noose
waiting. I'd have tossed it away
but I've learned to favor creation over
waste, to always opt for second life.

Thirteen

Her emotions ride inside
on a teeter-totter. Up. Down.
Glad. Sad. Twenty. Six.

She studies hard. Then refuses to.
She plays piano like a pro. Then
breaks into tears when I applaud.
She paints my old mailbox
to resemble a happy barn, then paints
her arms, her hands, her toes,
not noticing the prints she stamps
on the floor, the sink, the good
towel, yet she's so quick to change
when she finally sees the mess.

Good-natured. Sour. Bitter. Sweet.
She remembers everything
and when I haven't seen her
for a month or two, she's so much
bigger and even more beautiful
than she ever thought possible.

Sixty-nine

My emotions ride inside
on escalators. Sometimes
I still take the stairs.
Up. Down. Glad. Sad.
Eighty-nine. Forty-nine.

I am wise but refuse
to tweet, blog, text, friend or
unfriend and I can't remember
the simplest new instructions.
I paint the old woodwork
just one more time, then fall
asleep at eight watching
my favorite show. I'm fun,
then grouchy. Edgy, then I listen
intently to everything my grandchild
says. When she slips and falls, I'm
first to find the right bandage,
call the doc, tell her it will all be fine.

When the time between visits grows
long, she's touched by how I've slowed
down and how much more she loves me
than I ever thought possible.

The Old-Fashioned Treasure Hunt

Clue #1: **1014 100 2125: Look down and all around.** Right off, Gretchen knew, her 10-year-old brain fresh, active, no speck of cognitive despair like mine, 70. *Minecraft?* she whispered. *What?* I replied, dumb as any grandparent could be, but already she was plying her computer, which promptly paid out

Clue #2: **Under the reading by the throne, all alone.** I prayed for insight but couldn't offer much. The computer squealed: Gretchen's parents, Skyping from vacationland. *A toilet can be a throne*, she told them. *I'm stuck*, she said. Her voice held a complete puzzle. *Sleep on it*, Papa replied. His Skyped smile swept the screen. I suggested she check under the basket in the bathroom, Jackpot! Dusty, yes, but my brain still worked.

Clue #3: **In the 7th letter's museum ...** We were both stumped, but I more than she. Another day, another Skype, and somehow she'd guessed that the "7th letter" (a,b,c,d,e,f,G) meant "Gretchen" (OF COURSE), and "museum" meant "art gallery." Until then I'd barely glanced at the schooled art taped across the hall wall, where, slipped behind the picture she'd drawn of HOME, hid

Clue #4: **Sorry, Mom. Hi Gretchen, Welcome back, Papa. If you like to whirl, give me a spin.** My brain let out a pathetic cry but I forced a nonchalant shoulder shrug. G-daughter grinned. *X Box!* Me? Still dumb as any grandparent could be. *That's what the X Box says*, she explained. I didn't understand until the next night when we watched Willy Wonka and the Chocolate Factory. G, already a few inches taller than the last visit, faced the TV. *X Box on*, she commanded. The screen lit up: Sorry Mom. Hi Gretchen. Welcome back, Papa. *Movie, play*, she commanded, and it did.

Clue #5: **Hard, easy, or scrambled inside ...** Two days earlier, after Clue 1, Gretchen already knew. We'd baked sugar cookies for the school sale. G found her favorite recipe on her iPad and we'd creamed the sugar, the butter, the two eggs. *What's this?* I asked holding up one of two eggs still in the carton. G said, *Oh, Papa blew it out.*

There's a piece of paper rolled up inside. It must be the prize. We shouldn't look. He'd be disappointed. My G-daughter, the brain-genius.

And so we didn't look until after we'd found all the clues, and after G had cracked the eggshell and read the note promising that she and one friend would get a 2-day trip to the inside water slide and her eyes danced just like any kid's would have 60 years ago and her Skyping parents looked like the world was perfect and I, as smart as any grandparent could be, didn't say one word about the set of answers my foresighted son left for me under the table by the bed just in case my brilliant young G-daughter might need a little extra help.

Taking Grandson to His Piano Lesson

I.
Brew a fresh cup of caramel coffee
Find a hot/cold mug that will fit in the car holder
Top cupboard, get step ladder from daughter's pantry,
Figure out how to open ladder, do not criticize yourself
When you discover how simple it is
NASA travel mug, white, looks new, price tag still on bottom, $24
Probably shouldn't use
Fill NASA mug with freshly brewed caramel coffee
Force lid when it doesn't screw on right
Collect kid, head for car, go back for unpublished book
You are proofing for friend
So you have something to do during the piano lesson
Do NOT take a chocolate chip cookie
Start car, turn it around, follow MapQuest, printed out by daughter
Because you don't have GPS.
Note it is only 2.439 miles and 7 minutes
Not the 19.616 miles and 30 minutes
For last night's soccer game in Heritage Park
Almost impossible to read street names and setting sun sharp
In your eyes coming home
Also names on MapQuest printout
In very tiny print, or not there at all

II.
Left on Woodsonia
Second exit at first roundabout
First exit at second roundabout
First right onto Hedge Lane Ter
Third exit at next roundabout
Left onto Meadow, left onto 57th, second house is piano teacher's
This part easy because grandson recognizes it,
Grandson probably could have directed Grandma all the way,
But Grandma's daughter chose a different path
So Grandma could avoid
The really scary roundabout over the main highway
Very thoughtful daughter

III.
Wait in car.
Open windows.
Push seat back as far as it will go
Take sip of coffee
Find napkin to clean up mess when coffee spills all over
Remove lid from mug, set aside, sip coffee leisurely
Reach in back seat for unpublished book
Discover it's the wrong set of papers, the ones already read
Start car to shut windows because of flies, which like caramel coffee
Open windows again to chase out flies
Shut windows
Watch two other kids leave house and climb into other car
Waiting at foot of drive
Shut car off
Start car again because it is too hot.
Check MapQuest to reverse procedure for drive home
Write down most likely possibility for exits to take on roundabouts
On return trip, no it is not necessarily obvious, and no it is not
As simple to reverse as the old-fashioned stop signs
Do not worry if these exits are not clear in your mind
Be patient
You will get home on intuition

IV.
Start poem
Do not worry
When home, do not, repeat, do not
Eat chocolate cookie

V.
Grandson says piano lesson was good.

Thanksgiving Pome 2019

Home for the holidays, the girls, lanky in crisp jeans, long
sweaters, long wavy hair, stir the green beans. Their engineer
father (he plans to assume kitchen duties after he retires)
manages the meal, delegates the jobs, mine setting the table,
which my daughter's already mostly done, orange and red
seasonal harvest beneath Lenox, used all these years for
special occasions. She tells me they'd discussed ironing
the cloth, said I'd have done it, but decided it'd look fine
full with food. The boys wander in. Wil, youngest, follows
the box directions for the stuffing. On the counter: cherry,
apple, two pumpkin pies, plus the eggless cupcakes Raya
(oldest, holes in the jeans) made earlier for her mother's
birthday. I bought carrot cake at the church bake sale then
added candles for my daughter's 51st, already yesterday.
As instructed, I set short forks left of each plate except long
forks for my spouse and son in-law and Tom, the nephew
on the in-law side whom I've just met. Tom now works
where Chris works. An engineer? I ask, but he says "no,"
names some fancy other title—manager, I think. Young.
When Chris carves the turkey, my spouse asks me to ask
him to save the bones for us. Several years back, he threw
them away. Now Dan always asks me to ask him to save
them for us, which, for one short moment I hesitate to do,
then do anyway. Happy Thanksgiving, after all. I slept in,
a rarity, but I arrived tired, with a cough, and am glad for the
reprieve. When I finally drag myself up, I check the window
overlooking the backyard. The fancy multi-level kids' playset
has disappeared since my last visit. Grass, a yellower shade,
covers the spot. I wonder which of the kids care, when they
will care, if they will ever. I miss it, that fancy playset and
those little hands which used to grab mine, the high-pitched
chatting, the total trust which I did nothing to earn back then.
Wil calls from the other room, hearing his mother, sister,
and grandmother at the kitchen table. His voice sounds like
his brother's, and his brother's (I'd noticed) sounds like
their father's. Details push forward, prominent in this pome,
but I can't help noticing how even the "e" gets rearranged.

Fifteen

Tomorrow the braces
my granddaughter has worn
on her teeth for the past four years
will finally come off.
This morning, she slept late,
then spent the rest of the day
lounging in white terrycloth pajamas
with a hood that made her
look like an over-sized rabbit.
All afternoon she labored
on a speech she will give
in a mock trial in a real courtroom
with a real judge and a jury
made up of real attorneys.
My granddaughter will play
the defense attorney.
After supper, she exchanged
her bunny sleeper
for a stunning new pantsuit
and spiked heels, carefully
styled her shoulder-length hair
then practiced the opening argument
she will present next Saturday,
putting perfect polish
on a presentation
any professional lawyer
would be proud to claim.

Requests

Angels, seen or unseen,
Blessings, heard or unheard
Cash when needed
Death when necessary, though preferably painless,
Ease in old age
Faithful friends
invincible Hope, particularly in times of despair
enough Intelligence to learn to share
enough Joy to be able to share
enough Kisses to want to share
unconditional Love
healing mysterious inspiring majestic Music
Newspapers and the ability to read them
Openness and the luck to find it
a few good Prayers from those who care
occasional Quiet
understanding Relatives
Stars, 'specially
on a clear night with a loved one also watching
Toys to play with, even after childhood,
Usefulness, a positive sense of,
fresh Vegetables and the desire to eat them
Wisdom when you least expect it
X-rays that come back negative
Yodeling—how do they do that anyway?
a great Zoo along with a beautiful spring day to visit it
and also (how easy it is to forget) Gratitude
for Zest, Yea-sayers, Xenias, Wizards, Vitality,
Utopias, Trees, Songs, Rain, Questions, Parents,
Openness, Novelty, Magic, Lilies-of-the-valley,
Knowledge, Jokes, Imagination, Health, Grace,
Forgiveness, Eyesight, Dessert, Children, Birds,
Animals and even Alphabets

How to Have Real Fun and Enjoy It Too, In Hindsight

I. Jump rope, swing, twirl on the lawn
until you're so dizzy you drop. Play jacks, solitaire.
Read *The Bobbsey Twins*, pet the dog, practice piano,
collect marbles. Hide and seek in the hay mow.

II. Sleep over with friends, drive the tractor, get
your license, shop for a prom dress (more fun than the prom),
neck (sort of fun), get good grades (fun after the fact).
Read the *Ladies Home Journal* fiction series about the love
life of Henry VIII's last wife. Croquet.

III. Buy a house, fix it up. Rent a condo on the beach
for a week with friends. Build sand castles with the kids.
Read mysteries. Rock babies. Take walks, baths, trips.
Bridge, chess.

IV. Own a brand new red car, even though he paid for it,
not you. Buy more houses. Decorate more houses.
Buy make give gifts you think they'll like. Sit in the grass.
Jazzercize. Racquetball. Read stories you wrote to your
writing group. Invite company over for dinner
(fun when everything's finally ready).

V. Sex. Read poems you wrote to your lover. Take walks
with the dog. Buy your own car, even if it's not new.
Publish your first book.

VI. Hold hands with your husband. Eat popcorn, M&Ms,
hotdogs at the movies. Talk openly with your adult children
(who really seem to like you now). Talk openly with anyone
interested. Instant chats with family. Garden (with restraint).
Read a stack of 1970s *Better Homes and Gardens* which you
bought for a dollar at a garage sale, wonder how you
could have thought all that stuff was so great, hope you'll
get fresh insight, maybe a spiritual epiphany. Teach solitaire
to your granddaughter. Give away some of the marbles.

Great-Grandmother's Legacy

When my first dog dies, you paint
my fingernails apple red
and hold me in your lap until I feel better.

When I get married, you clean
the windowsills upstairs in my old bedroom
just in case someone happens to look.

When my father dies way too early,
you turn him into an icon who did no wrong
and loved me more than anyone.

When the grandchildren are born, you
crochet blankets for each even if
your arthritic fingers hurt.

When the divorce occurs, you pretend
you don't notice and that I am still
your amazing, brilliant daughter.

When I remarry, you like the new man
even better than the first one
regardless of how you really feel.

When life is hard, you hide your tears
because mothers don't burden their daughters
with unpleasant realities.

When you die, you tell me you
aren't going to make it this time
but that I will be okay anyway.

Hard Decisions

The next grandbabies I hold in my arms
will be my great grandbabies, not you,
dear grandchild who never knew Earth's charms.

Today, my youngest, my bonus baby,
the one who did not move out-of-state,
who always claimed you as a "maybe,"

reads my short history of grandmothering,
then requests I add my ode to you, unborn progeny,
a desire that left me softly sad and wondering

how to tell how the only thing I wanted
more than I wanted you was how to help
your awesome mother stay full and undaunted.

Marbles

When I was a kid
I was a pretty good shooter.
For a girl.
I collected hundreds,
kept them in the old tin candy box
Dad gave Mom when they were courting.
When I married, I hung on to them,
who knows why, maybe
for my own kids.
Dropped them one by one like memories
into a clear jar and set them
on the window ledge.
They went through several houses
that way. Colorful. Preserved.
All my marbles watching my life
from that perch by the sun.

Eventually my kids discovered them,
Fingered them fascinated, the way I once
sorted Mom's button box.
Old games—button boxes, marbles.
But passé. My kids grew bored,
Didn't know a cat's eye
from an immy, didn't care.
They flung them into forgotten corners,
slipped them down registers,
punched them into cracks in the car.
I rescued as many as possible,
hid them back of the cornstarch
on a high kitchen shelf.
Overnight they blossomed
into antiques. Just when I forgot
how to tell a rainbow
from a moonstone, someone
who loves me gave me three of his.
Special. Ancient. Rare.

Lullaby

Rock, rock, little one.
Lay your head on my breast.
Rest.

My sheltering arms embrace you
that the heat of my pulse
may warm you
and blanket your fall.

Rock-a-bye, baby, in the treetop.
When the wind blows …

Alas, tiny child,
sweet security lies! So soon
grown, infant innocence
blown with the wind.

Rock-a-bye, baby, in the treetop
Rock-a-bye, baby, so the moment
shall stop.

So soon you are three. Too big
then for me? So soon you are four.
More.

So fast it is you who sits
in my chair. My turn too fair,
too swiftly bare.

To and fro.
Back and forth.
The sway of life
beats a steady course.

Rock, rock, little one.
Lay your head on my breast
and let the waves of time
be stilled.

For Rob on Father's Day

Back in that math class where we met
I was caught by your big feet, big hands,
by the dimples appearing and disappearing
so mysteriously at smile's edge.
They tickled my fancy, those dimples.
Such a funny word—fancy. Archaic,
obsolete, like the love we shared back then
over coffee at Isaly's on High Street.
Remember how we roamed the city
that first year, collecting pop bottles
for coins to wash our laundry? When our girl
was born, she waited three endless, extra weeks
then arrived on your birthday, a gift to us both.
During that long watch, you laid your lips
where my stomach bulged out
and sang to her even then. You sang to her
for years, and to the two who came later,
miniatures beside you on the piano bench
while your strong lean fingers crossed the keys
and your voice rose above
the music of your hands, singing
> you're a pink toothbrush
> I'm a blue toothbrush
> Won't you marry me in haste?

and other crazy tunes.
I remember best those corny ones
> I'll be true, toothbrush
> Just to you, toothbrush
> When we both use the same toothpaste

for they made me laugh through those years.
A good show, I said, but later, after we both
started our second marriages, I saw that life
is all a show, and if it is good, like with you
during those years, then I am one of the lucky
who reap the harvest of weathered love.

The In-Laws Help

I.
Casual pleasantries in an Ohio park.
You shook my hand, a German custom?

II.
Packed possessions scattered like snow
along the hot summer highway.
Oh, no, we laughed, glad no one was hurt!

We lived together in a small trailer that summer,
You, me, your three-year-old granddaughter,
and your unborn grandson, looming large
whenever I walked. His dad would join us later,

would be there in time for his birth. But you?
Already back in Florida.

III.
For those two months, and long after,
there was crème de cacao on crushed ice
        I remember how you smacked the cube
        with a knife handle until your hand
        held frozen crystals, a simple task
        which I never could duplicate
served over Scat cards.
Loud "Karumbas," knuckles to table.
Guava jelly snacks.
Applesauce mixed with cottage cheese.

IV.
When you left, my own mother filled in.
No lingering for *this* baby. He was there,
perfect, before his dad could even unpack
his briefcase, anticipating a different wait.

My In-Laws Help Again

Taped letters,
yearly visits,
long walks,
late talks,
MacNamara's band
and a piano we helped you buy.

I was sick, remember?
You brought tea and blankets,
were quick to come when I,
confined to bed, needed help
with the first two children
in preparation for the not-so-easy
birth of the third child,
your last grandchild,
our bonus baby,

and between births, walks, talks,
and all the memories pasted in my mind
like pictures in an album,
lies more than ever shows
in black and white
or brilliant Kodacolor.

Named for Both Sides of the Family

Willi was the brightest, cutest, dearest,
most endearing, finest, grandest,
happiest, most innovative, jolly,
kindest, loving, sweetest, smartest,
most talented, upbeat son anyone
could ever, ever ask for,

but, of course, we never let on.

Perfume

Little girl in short white dress
dotted with colored hearts

how you jangle plastic bracelets
of hearts that match those hues

skip along the sidewalk singing
songs imperfect-pitched

your joy so selflessly distilled,
incense upon the air.

Just Once in My Life

Three nights ago
my daughter swallowed a quarter:
it hung in her esophagus for two hours
until the surgeon we never met
arrived, gowned, scrubbed, operated,
and freed her of the offensive coin,
which he presented us afterwards
as though a souvenir from Wall's Drug.

Right before the operation
my husband, breathing gin and tonic,
hurried inside. He'd eaten
only his dinner salad before the note came
to call the emergency room
and do not be alarmed.
White weariness curtained him.
He'd worked late all week
at a job he hates.
He stroked her hand, she, sitting
so straight on the hospital bed,
waiting … her seven-year-old eyes hurting
already for already she knew how guilt aches.
My husband passed me a glance,
moved his lips, fainted.

Nurse brought a chair, two chairs, brewed
coffee and offered it up in white paper cups.
One, in green, talked to her, too shrilly,
I thought. *I'll be with you. I'll be
your substitute mommy.*
My daughter's eyes curled down.
I want my real mommy and daddy.

Thank God it went well.
An hour after she awoke my husband
carried her to my car. I stuck the quarter
in my purse. She was sick all over
my jacket on the way home.

We put her to bed gently, as though
she were just born, and we never did
eat supper that night—we just went to bed
and in the morning my husband went to work
again, and today, I went to work again, and
my daughter went back to second grade and

tonight
I   work   late
only really I don't.
Really I sit silent in my office
where the ceiling fan whistles non-stop
(there are no windows) thinking
about an old love and how for a few months
just once in my life I'd felt not quite so
                                        alone.
I'm lucky, perhaps not everyone
gets to feel that way. Not even once
                              before,
a few years ago on a family trip
she'd swallowed a penny. We rushed forty
miles for x-rays. It passed through that time.
Last fall she swallowed a nickel riding
the school bus home. It passed through too.

A penny, a nickel, now a quarter.
Already we begin to joke.

Going to Mother's on Her Eightieth Birthday

Hour after hour for 936 miles
according to Triple A motor club.
It would be monotonous
if it weren't so relaxing.
Ten below wind chill factor and fresh
snow on the ground when my daughters
and I left Omaha yesterday. By
Fort Worth the Nissan is a mobile sauna.
Thank goodness my oldest likes driving,
I have slept more on this trip than I have
for months. Otherwise we pass time
at the Restaurant at the End of the Universe,
Conferring with the Moon: this is a New
Age, Mother. My daughters and I talk
about everything, everything except
that my-son-their-brother isn't sharing
this once in a lifetime occasion, so much
bitterness in divorce.

For your birthday, I write you
a poem, Mother, then tear it up
because it isn't good enough. I should
have written one sooner. Would have
but there wasn't time
or inspiration life has been hard
recently. Once long ago I wrote a poem
Going to Church on Easter
about a family, our family.
You wore smiles for days.
Back then you wore pill-box hats
with silk flowers and soft pink gloves
that reached to your elbows. Surely
the very pair I gave you for another
birthday. Back then you wrapped
my hair around rags, are still
wrapping my hair around rags, will always be
wrapping my hair around rags,
wearing long pink gloves.

Today I measure the distance
separating us in miles, file it under codes:
different generations, souls, perspectives.
Eighty is almost twice me.
Are you twice as wise, Mother?
Does it help, those extra years?
Or are they, like the distance separating us,
just an illusion? In the back seat
my youngest, your youngest urges me on.
You *can* write a poem, she says.
Just keep it short.

Last night in the motel there was no squabbling
about who would sleep with whom,
never before such a trip! Decisions
cost, yet there *are* compensations. At
Willies 305 Truckstop & Cafe in Temple
Texas I ponder buying a T-shirt
for my son, decide not to.
The graffiti on the restroom walls
reads Calamity Jane is a sleazy
slut. My oldest says You're a goon,
Mom. She means for writing
graffiti in my poem. What
does she know? She is only a fourth
your age. I have been in a thousand
restaurants like this one, even the waitresses
look the same. My youngest asks
what a goon is. The oldest explains:
someone who does crazy and fun things.
This is reality, reality at its prime.
This is getting my hair wrapped in rags
again. This is heritage. This is why
I am driving 936 miles to tell you it took.
The pink gloves. The smiles about poems.
The being a foundation.

Grieving

Cleaning copper in the kitchen, supper cooking,
oldest child home from college, middle suddenly
civil, third pouring vinegar, helping scrub moldy

green from the tray Mother gave us the first year,
from the pan always used for eggs, from the teapot
he bought four months ago, just before he left

for another life, then she the youngest the last
our babe says "it's easier to scour when you don't
work so hard at it," and even the dog is sad.

One Day I Came Home and Heard a Man in My House

I'd never heard before
though he'd been there
for years. Still, I gasped

when I opened the front door
found that voice, that low
throaty laugh

trickling down the stair
into my ears
like a Polaroid picture

developing while I watched,
that new deep sound
charging the air, blinding me

to the familiar, mundane
shape of his *Hi Mom, how
was your day?*

When the Last Child Leaves Home

Everything shifts.
The dog mopes.
The house grows bigger, the walls suddenly speak.

You and your spouse sit on spotless sofas, eat fancy
dessert, remind each other diligently how she's
been gone lots of nights before. Then you say

it's different now.

What comes next?
Some of the answers sting, so you shut your mind,
call on the dead cat's ghost to reassure, find faith

in tiny acts of creation, the womb of metaphor
wondrously not yet dry, pray this one small gift

of birth won't go too.

The Old Dollhouse

Goes,
along with the just-graduated daughter,
now moving to a different city
a different home
a different set of dishes.

Born
from a neglected china cabinet
converted, when she was three,
into nine toy rooms.
Each birthday, Christmas,
something new added
behind glass doors, why
you could see
the whole dollhouse world
at one quick glance.

I dust
away cobwebs, tears,
glimpse her life with me,
a little girl who held my hand
while we moved from city to city,
house to house, child to young
woman who arrives soon
in a U-haul truck
to cart away this tiny universe,
now turned into her own.

Graduation Song

You stand now across the way, amidst
cars and moving vans, ready to travel
alone. It's a long stretch from the day

we first rode home together, me
still in shapeless maternity clothes,
you wrapped in the mint green shawl

your grandmother crocheted with love
and arthritic fingers and welcome.
When you left a few years back to live

with your father, I stared at the few artifacts
that stayed behind. A picture you painted
in the third grade. Old school reports.

Memories. On the bulletin board above
my desk I pinned a florist's card—on it
your scribbled signature and *Happy*

Mother's Day. And I cried out in protest,
for the road seemed steep and unyielding.
Soon you were wearing man shoes

and when you returned for an overnight
or a few days or Christmas you brought
with you grown-up clothes, a plastic razor,

a new openness which you wore handsomely.
I see more clearly now. You are again
a little boy, practicing endless magic tricks.

Yet separate roads are sleight-of-hand.
Illusions! Clever, magnificent illusions!
Go safely, son. You need not fear the way.

You travel the familiar avenue of life.
Make your own music. But keep this song
to guide you and to know that all is one.

Reflections on Doing Nothing
(for Sonna)

Nothing tops doing nothing.
But if you're the addictive
sort—compulsive,
perfectionistic, workaholic,
Type A, overachieving, over
dedicated, over-zealous, doing
nothing is climbing Mt. Everest
with crippled feet
or flying an airplane
without any fuel
or stopping the rain
the day you planned
a garden party. Doing nothing
takes willpower and more
imagination than a three-legged
hog hobbling into church.
Doing nothing requires a steel cold
glare when someone stalks
into the room where you are
doing nothing, smiles meaningfully,
and asks what are you doing?
And if that someone carries
an armload of groceries
or a sweeper or a rake
or an infallible expression,
doing nothing needs a weapon
more devastating than hot nuclear
fusion—the truth. Keep your
cold glare, if you wish, but
insist firmly, flatly, that you
are doing nothing and that you
are working hard at doing nothing
because, if you're not
careful, you will wind up
doing something and then
you will never
ever get nothing done.

Blessings from the Bride's Mother
(for Sonna and Chris)

Three may your blessings be.

First, roots to hold you close,
To love and nourish you
To anchor you on dangerous cliffs
      To center you through pain and disappointment
      To support your every effort
      To remind you who you are

Second, wings to set you free
      To guide your future path
      To soar with joy
      To discover the tulips hidden in the sky
      To help you search for Truth
      To show you who you can become

Roots.
Wings.

Roots and wings together.

And, third,
faith to accept such contradictions.
Faith.
For then your individual lives
will each radiate hope
and your wedded life will be rich
with mystery
and peace.

A Found Poem

Forasmuch as Wil and Kathleen
have thus pledged themselves each to the other
in the presence of this company,

by virtue of the authority vested in me
by church and state, I now pronounce them
husband and wife.

And inasmuch as I am also Wil's mother
and have therefore a very special feeling
about this marriage, I want to express

my gratitude for the privilege
of officiating at this ceremony.

Kathleen, I welcome you as my daughter.
Wil, I promise not to offer you
too much motherly advice. This occasion

makes me sing in my heart.

How to Make a Mean Cat Like You
("Enhanced" Version)

Sabina—long-haired, calico—loved Mindy
despite the monthly baths, but hated Mindy's
boyfriend from Day 1. P.C., a giant man, naturally
good-natured, offered catnips, treats. *Here, kitty!*

Sabina looked nails at him, hissed when he tried
to touch her, began growling even before Mindy
opened the door, P.C. always waiting outside
with long stems.

After a year and no change, P.C. wanted to marry
Mindy. Mindy's mother said something must be wrong
with a man a cat didn't trust. Nonsense, Mindy said.
Mindy threw pillows at Sabina when she hissed at P.C.

P.C. read up on cat behavior, fanned yarn before Sabina.
Sabina wasn't playing. Mindy considered selling Sabina.
Sabina nuzzled Mindy, placed a paw softly on her face,
purred. But whenever P.C. arrived, Sabina's back arched
and her tail shouted. One day, Sabina hurled herself at P.C.
from the refrigerator top, dug declawed paws into his neck.
Instinctively, P.C. grabbed, flung her across the room.

Hsss, Sabina said.

I don't get it, P.C. complained. His shoulders slumped.
The next day he brought Mindy a present which he carried
in a red canvas box with a see-through door. Grinning broadly,
he zipped it open. Out jumped a large Persian cat
with shaved body, full mane, bushy boots, a huge, fluffy tail.

Meet Tiger, P.C. said.

Sabina hid for three days,
But on the fourth, the day P.C. gave Mindy a gold ring,
Sabina and Tiger lay side-by-side in the round basket
by the heater.
Mew, Sabina said.

My First Husband Visits after Twenty Years

The brunch is in honor of our youngest
child's wedding. The house is the one where
the kids mostly grew up. My ex and I bought
it together after a job change and subsequent
cross-country move. It's Sunday, early enough
that out-of-towners can still make their flights.
My second husband—who years ago added
the half-bath on the first floor for my late mother
and who built the porch last summer—greets
guests at the front door. My ex and I once took
that same door to a wood stripper, left it
a natural oak. Months ago, I painted it spring
green. The kin of my life—our three children,
five grandchildren, in-law siblings and cousins,
my own cousins, assorted spouses—check out
the feast on the kitchen island that wasn't even
there when my ex lived in the house. Two couples,
friends of my second marriage, prepare the brunch,
serve it, clean up after, bear witness to this strange
event. One whispers how my ex studied every
thing in the house. If I were he, I'd do the same
and I'd probably try to do it when he wasn't
watching, too. My current husband—gracious,
supportive—disappears somewhere, maybe
upstairs in the library with my daughter's new
in-laws here from Italy just for the occasion.

We've been married, my husband and I, nearly
as long now as my ex and I were. We are growing
old, all of us. My husband has a cold that doesn't
seem to go away and a lump in his lungs that
worries me. Later, after the brunch, my kids will
tell me how their dad exited the plane yesterday
with pain in his chest. He took an ambulance to ER,
but he was fine, just too much caffeine, too little
sleep. I'm teary as my ex and I say goodbye. He
gives me a short but genuine hug, the first since

that time when I told him about my new love and
he nearly drowned me (unintentionally of course)
in a large, serene lake a long, long way away.

Sestina

My daughter, psyched by an assignment from her class,
claims the form is numerological: one, two,
three, four, five, six—the pattern folds over three
times in each new stanza, six to one, five to two, four
to three. It's confusing as hell, well, give me five,
I know that's trite and superficial, but the point is six

months ago she turned fundamentalist, six
short months to unwrap twenty-one
years of motherly shaping, and now, at fifty-five
I find myself afraid to swear in front of her, too
conscious of the ramifications flowing before
us like the big bad wolf's wind blowing down three

pig houses. I huff and puff infinity times three,
plus a reiterating constant, come up with six
googols full of pure B.S., plenty for
one lifetime. I'm a minister. I should have won
this war long ago. Okay, so she's twenty-two,
not twenty-one, I forget things I knew five

minutes ago, just like my own mother. No, it's five
seconds for her, she who's going on ninety-three
since two Tuesdays ago, but thinks its still ninety-two,
or a hundred and seven, or maybe only eighty-six.
She's old, Mother is. She's a survivor, one
ready to cash in her chips (her phrase), to go before

her Maker, but, meantime, ready each afternoon by four
o'clock for the evening supper that's not until five.
And then … sundowners, the only constancy one
can count on in assisted living. That and three
meals offered every day until death, ready or not. Six
times she's seen the doctor already since the dawn of Two

Thousand, the age of Aquarius. Of Compassion. Too
soon to tell. My mother swears. Damn, she says. For-

tunately, no one hears but me. Maybe it keeps the evil 666
away? There **is** purpose in blasphemy. My daughter, at five,
knew—and did—the boy next door making three
for two sleds, and only her cursing stopping him, one

stunned fourteen-year-old kid going on two. Five
times I've told this story from the pulpit; a parable. Three
folks got it. Six misunderstood. My daughter, another one?

Velvet Costumes and the Period Art Project

Flatland people wear paper doll clothes
pass their entire lives
on opposite sides of a patched city street
where miniature businesses, houses hug
the background in primary hues.
Blue. Yellow. Red.
But the man with the work hat
and the girl hurrying home a bagged bottle
of booze are born of black cardboard
and my twenty-year-old's twenty-first century
imagination.

"Please," they beckon, "join us."

We hesitate. Their world
is too planar for our blood and bone bodies.
No velure. When we try to enter, we see
only our own narrow limitations,
normally hidden in three dimensions,
now dangling from wire hangers,
tabs exposed, waiting for us to claim them
as our own.

Portrait by an Unknown Girl

Saturday afternoon. Doorbell. Tiny girl
peddles her art. My daughter, no longer
tiny anymore, answers the ring, studies

the picture proffered—a slim, faceless girl
with straight brown hair and no elbows.
Yellow skirt, shirt. Belly button bared.

Her big-heeled shoes, pointed out, are
executed in shades of pastel yellow, all
delicately penciled within the designated

boundaries. The canvass, an ordinary sheet
of lined school paper, bears bold flourishes
under black block letters imperfectly

centered at the top. "Fashion Clothes." Un-
signed but not untitled. Moments of intense
bargaining, a satisfactory three cents

is agreed upon, exchanged. Shortly after,
I am gifted with this amazing prize portrait,
framed and hanging years later even now

on my office wall, a fundamental part
of a growing gallery of penetrating
renditions on the feminine mystique.

My Son Sent Flowers

On a leisurely September walk
I pass multi-hued impatiens,

park roses abloom, grass green
again after the recent cool.

By the sidewalk, weeds wait
uprooted, clumped, abandoned.

I bend, tuck a few long stems
not yet shedding into otherwise

empty hands. New: age spots dot
the hands that carry crisp leaves

still stuck to re-envisioned stalks.
On my way home I discover wisps

of dried wheat, two still-red branches
for my bouquet. One twig hangs

determined, reluctant to separate.
In my yard, I cut purple geraniums,

blue petunias, phlox, the single orange
mum, trailing ivy, baby's breath.

Inside I finally toss flowers my son
sent three weeks ago, salvage

the eucalyptus, add my new finds,
stand back, admire the life scent.

Prime Rib

Fresh from the freezer where the women stashed it
after wrapping each piece in slick white water-proof paper,
a day-long task made easier by conversation and many hands,
even mine as soon as I was old enough.
I remember the cold, squishy feel of raw hamburger, a mix
between playing in sand and in mud, only much better
—the strong red meat smell something you never forget.

We named all the milkers back then, but Dad was careful
never to specify which one the butcher got, just in case.
We always saved the prime rib for special occasions
like Christmas or visits from Aunt Fern's city family,
all of us gathered about Mom's fine cherry-wood table
extended to full capacity by six hand-hewn boards.

Last week we gathered around that same table
at my daughter's new house, used part of the ten-place
dish-set Mom gave me when she moved to the Home,
and I gave to my daughter for her wedding, but kept
tucked away until she finally moved someplace with space.
And there we were Saturday, table topped with fine linens
and autumn-pink leaves etched into now-antique
white china rimmed with gold, and all that top-of-the-world
happiness permeating my daughter's dining room.

New Sheets on My Daughter's 50th Birthday

Mother used to say
that if she were rich
she'd have fresh sheets
on her bed every night.

In her day, the best bed
cloths were those hung
In the sunshine to line dry,
nothing ever quite matching

that crisp, bleached smell.
When I was little
she still ironed her sheets
once each week, and before

that she ran them through
an iron mangle with a huge
round tube which smoothed
them perfectly flat.

She stored them in the closet,
edges neat, and used tight
hospital folds on the corners
when she made up her beds.

Mother was born in 1908,
I was born in 1945, and Sonna,
firstborn, was born in 1968.
It is likely that Sonna

has never slept on sun-
bleached sheets. Or on starched
sheets in the winter. Cultures
change at the flick of an invention,

fitted, wrinkle-free percale
bedding being something
Mother knew only late in her life
but my daughter has always

known. She and her neighbors
who all live in lovely large homes
filled with children, activity, hope
—homes built on modest lots

where corn used to grow—
wash and dry their sheets
in clever laundries tucked
around the corner from their

comfortable master bedroom
suites. Today, on the eve
of Sonna's fiftieth birthday,
I decide to gift her

with a brand new set
of queen sheets, high
thread-count,
something special which

Mother would have coveted.
My daughter can select
from among the latest designs:
utopian bedding, brushed

velvety microfiber, hotel quality,
luxurious, extremely durable,
extra soft, deep pockets,
easy fit, breathable and cooling

sheets … all reasonably priced
quick access and delivery
online through Amazon,
my daughter's choice now

how to start this next
important part of her life.

August in Austinburg[1]

Television was pre-embryonic
when first I gazed
upon this symbol, this myth
we participate in. O Gaia,
frosted in green grass,
forest-ribboned, sprinkled
with sun-flowers, surely you,
as Campbell once purred,
are the landscape of the soul.

---

[1] In 1945, Austinburg, Ohio, was a small town of about 500 people. Today, it is almost 600, though the township has a 2020 population of 2,078.

Smelt

First, birthing
hospital   antiseptic   medicinal   bloody   unremembered,
                                             except for the smell

lingering … in subterranean planes,
galaxies I travel when no one interferes.

Second, the barn
so many, so pungent
cascading over each other like soup
whitewash   silage   manure   manger   metal
                          mixed seasonings swirled in milk

still raw warm and garnished
with animal flesh and   mine.

Outside,
dank, forest woods in the back lot
water   earth   snow   leaves   elderberries   wild timothy hay
and me
sitting on a leather seat,
circling
keeping watch while the baler gobbled green mounds,
coughed out loaves bound with twine.
When the sun sweltered, we stopped, drank ginger
(4T ginger, 24T sugar, 16T vinegar to every gallon)
water

Inside,
newly pasted wallpaper and furniture polish
Christmas trees and the powder Grandma dusted on her face
in front of the mirror
in the guest bedroom. Then

the red rouge of puberty. High school.
The long bus ride. Sister in college. Brother in the Navy. Alone,
                                             but not alone.

Last, the stench of sickness
the night my father died
there in the master bedroom
where I was conceived
even though Mother wasn't supposed
to have more children.

Onions.
Roses.

Farm Fugue

Once farming meant sweaty overalls,
muddy boots stashed by the woodshed door,
kids handling huge hazardous machinery,

Lyle yodeling, rinsing bottles in the milk house,
sandpaper tongues shoving iron levers in water bowls,
cows warm whenever I lay down beside them.

Once farming meant tasting grain, petting kittens,
holding buckets for newborn calves,
jumping from haymows, sculpting rooms

from tall grass, shaping angels in snow,
scraping horns with broken glass,
long solitary walks by the creek

and the cornfield

and the far north woods. Later,

>   big business possibilities,
>   bankruptcy concerns,
>   no one in the next generation
>   wanting to carry on

but once farming meant Daddy rising at four,
stoking the coal furnace til the kitchen register
sent hot blasts around my legs,

at seven Daddy stomping snow off wet galoshes,
hanging his smelly barn jacket by the back door,
morning chores already done.

Three Silos

I think that I shall never see
a sculpture quite so grand as these
great pillars towering high.
The first stands square; its age
is old. Amish made the second
rise, like Christ, in counted days.
The third remains a product
of the future of my youth, both doomed
to pass. And yet all live by artisan hand—
rare monuments to history's eye.

Things Daddy Would Never Tolerate

Some things Daddy just wouldn't abide.
Laziness. Rude children. Democrats.

Having his picture taken with other men
in such a way that his shortness showed.

Machinery that didn't work. Manure-
splattered whitewash, overflowing gutters.

Girls in the barn when the vet came. Men
who courted his daughters with liquor

on their breath. Women who smoked.
Unpolished shoes. Dishonesty. Being

paralyzed by a stroke. Dying anywhere other
than on the homestead he loved.

Still Standing There

Mother, do you remember
the kitchen of my roots?
New green linoleum.
Wallpaper on the ceiling
to hide plaster cracks.
Dad fashioning a tin shade
for the fluorescent light,
spraying it copper.
Me, standing on a chair,
long curls hanging over
the ledge, watching
your fingers shape rolls,
roll crusts, cut cookies.
I remember that lower left-
hand drawer where you
kept your spices. Now
a microwave sits where
your fancy two-oven
pull-out cook surface
Tappan range ought to be.
The cold pantry where we
stored old copies of *Life*
is a heated sitting room.
The worn countertops
you covered with "brick"
contact paper is sleek Formica.
But Mother, the cabinets are
exactly like they were
and you are still standing
there, wiping your hands
on your apron,
making that kitchen
ready.

My Mother's First Home

Dad drove forever, getting to Grandma's. In those days
no Freeway, only trucks that crawled so slowly Dad took
risks. Mother grew uneasy, my brother and sister impatient,
and me, invariably, car sick. We didn't make the trip often.
Mother would have liked to visit more.

It was worth it once we arrived. Grandma and Grandpa's
solid house (Grandpa built it himself) sat on Main Street
amidst cherry and apple trees he planted. He planted
a blue-ribbon garden, too. Grandma tended it.
At Grandma's, my sis and I slept in the "girls" room,
in the three-quarters bed where Mom and *her* sis once slept.
My brother slept on the sleeping porch if it was warm.
Our parents had the guest room with the strange,
hard-to-open desk Grandpa had handcrafted. Grandpa
and Grandma had side by side rooms. Grandpa snored.

Grandpa's room smelled of pipe. I rarely went in.
Grandma's room was all powder and perfume.
I loved to sit on her high bed, watching, talking.
Everything was tidy in Grandma's room, even
inside her bureau drawers. She had a kind of under-
shirt instead of a bra like Mother wore. Odd! Grandma
was thin and flat-chested, her breasts hardly bigger
than mine. Her closet held only dresses. Weekdays
she added an apron and on Sundays or visiting days,
a hat and gloves. Grandma dressed slowly, meticulously,
not minding me watching. She parted her thin, white hair,
then tucked it into a neat little twist where the back
of her head met her neck. Grandma saved everything.
Her rag bag hung by the basement stairs. Her button bag
and sewing basket sheltered in the dining room buffet.
Her kitchen cabinets held boxes filled with rubber bands
and plastic bags, all carefully rinsed, folded, stacked
by size. On the back porch sat her old wringer washer,
used every Monday. No, she didn't want one
of those modern ones. She just didn't, that's all.

Everything had its place at Grandma's.
Even she and Grandpa seemed to have their places—
his chair in the living room before the fireplace, his
and her chairs at the kitchen table. He sat by the radio.
She, by the door, usually with a pan of green beans
to snap or cherries to pit or, at least, her mending basket.
Grandma was short; she propped her feet on a wooden
footstool Grandpa made for her from part of a previous
laundry machine. The thin, gold-rimmed glasses
on the edge of her nose looked as fragile as she did.

I never thought of her as fragile, though. I thought of her
as strong. She knew so much. How to make perfect cherry
and apple pies, how to tell one flower from another,
how to humor Grandpa, how to entertain granddaughters
for hours on end. Just about everything.

As the years passed, Grandma grew funnier.
She couldn't remember things, asked the same question
ten times in a row. It bothered Mother, but I didn't mind,
not even when she couldn't claim my name anymore.
Mother fretted. Grandma began to wander at night.
She mixed up medications, didn't always turn the stove off.
Suddenly, another woman lived with them, a housekeeper.
Grandma and Grandpa needed someone to help them out,
Mother said. Between visits, Mother and Aunt Fern talked
often on the phone; one day they visited their parents together.
I was a teenager then, with activities. Also, I wasn't invited.
When Mother came home, she seemed sad. Grandma was
"living in a home, now." Once, I heard her talking to Dad
about how Grandma had to be tied in bed. Mother visited
more frequently, but she didn't ask me to go with her.
I never saw Grandma again, not until that last time
when she lay in her casket. Mother was sad, but relieved.
It had really troubled her, the being tied down part.

Mother is wrong when she thinks I don't remember
Grandma at her best. Her best had nothing to do with
not remembering or wandering at night or not being able

to cope. Grandma at her best was how she always made her granddaughter something precious, rare, special. No disease ever made that disappear, not even now.

I inherited Grandma's footstool. I painted it black and use it as a flower stand. Every time I look at it, Grandma says hello.

The Cost of a Medium-Sized Dog

for its lifetime—sixty-four hundred dollars
according to a sign posted in the bathroom stall
at the science museum in the city near the town
where my grandparents rest high on a steep, grassy hill
their graves upright in a cemetery of fine stones.

My Great Uncle Irving, dead before my birth, lies
next to his wife Bertha whom I might have met but didn't.
Great Uncle Art, the youngest, never married, always strange,
is buried right of Grandad, two over from Grandma.
I remember Uncle Art, his octagonal house, the kitchen

sink, cupboards all lowered to accommodate his ailing mother,
Grandad's mother, who raised all six children alone on the farm
after her husband deserted or something, no one ever told
not one word about this great grandfather whose tombstone
and name are conspicuous for their absence near

Great Grandmother Amelia,1845-1926, all facts
I didn't know yesterday, like the cost of my tears
as I stood before the family plot seeing, once again,
Grandma, Grandad, Uncle Art (who left it all to his church),
our whole family at the dining table by the yellow kitchen

in the house Grandad built years ago, long before that
red brick insurance agency rose in its place.
                                        At the science center
my husband and I watch a film about the great carnival of life
of coral reefs (the exact words), how global warming is causing

them all to die. A second film, about bugs, ends when the preying
mantis eats a butterfly. On another sign I learn how a dying person
loses sight, taste, smell, touch, hearing, in that order, and how
an ordinary pencil contains enough lead to draw a line
thirty-five miles long or to write fifty thousand words.

Not Everyone Can Ride a Bike

I drove a tractor before I mastered the bike,
then rode as if I balanced a pail of water
on a needle, my mission not to spill.

At twenty-two, I rode to save gas, headed
straight toward a sidewalk pedestrian,
swerved right, left, right again but still

collided. Her injuries, blessedly minimal;
her face, a Pulitzer for stunned.

Never again, the feel of wind washing my face
while my legs pedal circles of pleasure.

Patience

Every Sunday morning meant
cousin Cherie's hand-me-down
dresses and Austinburg Church
(the only one) and hour services
that stretched my imagination.
I made games: trying to keep up
with the responsive reading,
learning words to all four verses,
pretending church was done and
we'd stopped at the town bar
for the *Cleveland Plain Dealer*
and I was already sprawled out
on the dining room rug, studying
comics, smelling the only meal
Mother cooked on Sundays, aware
that later there'd be Roy Rogers,
popcorn. Yet I was ever certain
that after the big hand reached 12,
there'd be the hopping outside,
post to post to post, grownups
always talking, and only rain—
or baling—could alter the pattern
every Sunday morning meant

Picnic at Thompson Ledge

After Mom's chicken
and baked beans
(both wrapped in layers of newspaper),

we climbed down through cold,
damp rocks to the lighted space below
knowing that at the end of this brief journey

was the promise of adventure.
Caves. Lush carpets of moss. Ledges.
Ledges so unbelievably high

I had to hold tight to my brother's
hand so my breath couldn't escape,
leaving me gasping.

Another View of Those Maples

Picture them groomed
with tiny pipes,
buckets hung for sap,
whisking three youngsters
between them toward
the waiting yellow bus,
waving in the wind
Hello, goodbye, hello.

Picture all seven
silken with snow
or ripe with red.
Grand old dames,
these gossips.

What do you suppose
they whispered the day
that ugly new house
on the street's other side
came to eavesdrop?

Stained Glass

The past revisited is a door ajar.
I'd not seen this colorful front
entrance for twenty-five years, one
quarter century to brave this view
of someone else's artifacts.

Sometimes it takes two or three
lifetimes to dare knock again
at those tender openings, then
when we finally enter, everything
rushes at us together.
Cold ice cream and hot fudge sauce.

Cautiously we feel our way,
mistaking for intuition
those things imperfectly remembered,
saying out loud to ourselves
"The door's the same, but Good
Heavens, look at that wallpaper."

After

Speculation has it
that heaven is blue,
unfit for the rich.

Orphaned at 55,
I miss my parents,
wish time could yo-yo.

Long stretches of contact, conversation, communication,
                                          creative care disappear

in a flick of the wrist

then wind out again, a thin string of serial reruns, not quite fresh
                                                          but still satisfying.

Some expect rebirth,
an endless replay
until enlightenment.

As a child, I watched
my brother spin the spool
off his hand, reel it in again.

What came after is a length of certainty that, later, looks pivotally
                                                                      like magic.

The Gravel Road
(by the Omaha Home)

where else can you live
as close to a gravel road
as the one framing the farm
of my midwestern youth yet

still be smack in the midst
of a city filled with arts
music, math, metaphor
poetry, philanthropy, pride

pleasure
prayer

Stones Last

Everything changes. Houses change.
Jobs change. Husbands change.
Souls slip in and out of bodies

according to fashion. Truth
is relative. Alan Bloom's best
seller stops selling. Truth

is absolute. Plato stops fooling
around with little boys, time
is only a 4th dimension, and, yes,

I'm still lying about the stones.

Old, Full Baskets

In executive suit
of epic proportions,
rich in freedom
and American ease
like the ad read
when you ordered it
one lifetime ago
on your lunch break,
how confidently you
tore yourself out of
the magazine, Virginia Slim,
began coming a long way,
Babe,
not even noticing
the full apron
still wrapped
about your tailored clothes
with invisible ties,
binding you tightly
to pages past,
flat,
black, white.
When you board your bus
tomorrow morning, Virginia,
sweep your briefcase high;
bear it on your head
with dignity
and ride the wheels of change
sweetly, as the ancient soft hum
of women washing dirt
from their clothes
with smooth, worn stones.

Forty

Inside of me there burns
a passion
like those tiny candles
sometimes found on birthday cakes,
tricking
the unsuspecting
making momentary belief:
the flames put out at last,
the wish assured,
fulfillment one hot breath,
one warm embrace,
one kiss aired long
and aimed straight
for those mighty miniscule fires
quitting
at song's end, but then
surprise!
a joyful pause
turned
instantly to wonder
when the colors oxidized
flick back to life,
magical and ceaseless,
and every year
yet one more
added on.

Grandma's White Horses

Grandma Henderson always said she'd know her time
was up the day she saw the white horses coming.

Inside, I smiled at Grandma, set about getting through
the rest of my life as best I could, not wanting to be
anybody special, or so I once told an ex-priest,

not recognizing the lie. It didn't matter, my lying.
Ex-priests aren't very nice guys, at least not the one

I knew. My ex-priest coveted plattered turkey
on Christmas day with all the trimmings, like a wife
and a chance to be the father he'd never had, and me

except I already was a wife, bad news for ex-priests
even if they're radical. What could he do but tell me

to put him out of his life while he got on with his?
Once a priest, always a priest I suppose he believed
himself when he claimed, avoiding my eye, that we'd

known each other forever. So, a little inconvenience
like the rest of our lives? Life a gift and all. Fact,

I think now, but then life's gotten slippery lately.
My ex-priest keeps turning up in the oddest faces,
in the tiniest innuendos, in the worst moments.

Reality needs firm ground to stop it from shaking
or so I insisted right before he X'ed me out. I was

wrong: confusing reality with life is a fatal mistake.
I know better now I've begun to remember. Grandma's
horses, for instance. How when I was still quite young

I spent a night at Grandma's house. Outside the window,
hooves hitting the gravel hard, fast. I peeked behind

her curtain, scrutinizing night, seeing nothing. As they
galloped past, the floor vibrated wildly, vibrates yet
as old years roll by, leaving me wondering.

The Church, the Stone, and the Grass Widow

Recently I've tried
a Congregational, a Presbyterian, one fundamentalist,
a few high masses. Twice a priest presented me
a thin white wafer and a sip of red juice.
I surprised myself by crying. My latest church
is small and struggling, but the minister, newly ordained,
newly divorced, newly installed, is friendly
and the congregation needs members maybe even me.

Recently I've tried
astrology, graphology, energetics, tarot, and a psychic
shrink. The psychic saw a puppy dog in my future,
neglected to tell me it would get hit by a car, cost $400
at the vet's. The energy healer said I'd been programmed
six centuries back for a miserable life, but it was okay
now because I could be reprogrammed. The card reader
saw the Fool in my immediate future, my handwriting
revealed clear signs of family strife dating back
to my childhood, the astrologer said he was a romantic
at heart but even he could offer no hope, absolutely
not one chance, for my marriage to work, it was all right
there in my chart.

Recently I've tried
a new job, lover, furniture arrangement
(after my husband moved out),
three new shrinks, and a hairdo. The hairdo
and the lover helped most, the hairdo because it
made me feel attractive and the lover because he
gave me a stone which he called Wisdom
and which he said would guide and protect me
and be my friend forever and ever amen,
rock of ages, I put it on a chain, wear it
around my neck as a sure sign of resurrection.

Songs of Tomorrow

Tonight the radio plays
an eerie lullaby,
the kind
that belongs to Halloween spook houses
or incense-laden rooms
draped with beads, rustling with tapestries.
The sound cushions me from the emptiness
of my changing life—did Mother,
cradling me in her arms,
dare suspect this future?
Mother is old now, and distant. I wonder,
as she readies herself for her days
of playing bridge and visiting her dying husband
and playing bridge,
does she hum under her breath and are
the words "You made your bed lie in it"?
Wondering, I fear
the hidden song of my heart.
Has it, too, become cynical and bitter, this divorce
more than a marriage broken? The only
difference between Mother and me
that I admitted it? Emptiness unseen
a walking dirge?

Life scored in twenties. Twenty years
of Mother, twenty of marriage.
When my husband left he took
his violin and mandolin,
the piano, the tape deck, the tapes
and the newer records. He left two
radios, the record player with
the broken needle.
Tonight, I feel
the familiar pull of a softer, more urgent melody.
Tomorrow, early, I will do something noteworthy.
Like cleaning out the garage; maybe
I'll even sing
while I work.

Metamarriage

If I could hold it in my hand like a crystal Christmas ball,
I'd gaze and gaze, entranced by the subtle hues, ever changing.

How the tides of our entangled histories rise and fall within!
Storms swirl, clouds protect newborn suns and the old

faithful star flickers intermittently, always lit by memories
collected. O living ornament, your mirror veneer reflects

my awe at your rarity. Just breathe, precious jewel, and I will
hang you high with my ribbon words, that all may marvel.

Violets

Now in the springtime of my old age
there is a newness to things,
in things

in the death of Uncle Dick
who was my children's uncle
instead of mine

in the grey threads
sewn boldly
into my hair

in the smell of grandparent
covering my lover
like violets blanketing
fresh-thawed ground
and scenting the air

in this world of speeding sun-turns
and mutual sounds
and infant awareness
I reach for the low red
branches on the tree
of consciousness
and begin to pull myself
upright.

Umbrella Dance in Chocolate Time

Walking in rain, hunting for a phone
trying to keep my feet dry suddenly
he was there beside me holding an ugly
umbrella, grey and white with a touch
of red mathematics, he'd found it abandoned
in a classroom. He appeared in full costume,
disguised as five decades Irish Catholic only
the frayed collar tipped me off. Under
the cleansing mists we walked and talked,
saying little, as though we were lovers,

how we hadn't the hang yet of matching
motions, how it was a dance, how frankly I
was always a wall-flower. I followed
the umbrella. He led. We tapped time
to "I Have Often Walked Down This Street
Before" but I didn't recognize the road
now it was paved and besides all those
sycamores doing their own rain dance
overhead, then this world of masquerade
where only the chocolate is real
moved, maybe he caused it?

Truth is I follow pretty well when
someone guides. And he promised.
The trick is to believe he wants to
and can. Here they call it trust. I say
thank you, I'd love to. Finally found
the phone, called a tow for the car
broken down one tune ago, made it back
before the truck arrived and he held me
in his arms as though it were an ordinary day.

Exactly

What do you mean exactly
when you urge me
to believe in the moon
even when it is not seen?
What do you mean exactly
when you speak of love
and call me the thread
which ties it all together?

You will stitch your way
into my heart
with your pretty
empty words

I will be so awed
by the color of your designs
that it won't matter
if you drop a stitch
here and there
or if you miss the pattern
now and then

for the pattern is not mine
nor yours

It is sewn in the sky
like stars on a flag,
and even when it is not seen
it hangs on the moon,
waving in the wind,
exactly as it was meant to be

Second Chance

Prepare yourself, Love! The carpet cleaner's
here and I ordered new covers for the couch
I bought with husband number one.

I washed and *ironed* curtains, bleached all
household smells. The windows need some
elbow grease and we'd better paint the hall.
A basement sale should help the clutter.
Could you finish off that downstairs bath?
insulate the walls? repair the drooping ceilings?
replace that rotten board? and would you fix
that broken shutter on the west side of the house?
Then I'd like to buy a picture that is "ours."
This place must look just right for what

I have to say. Love, my dog and child like you,
the way a woman loves her house,
a bachelor guards his solitude,
the toothpaste creeps outside the cap.
I like you, the way the cat likes the sofa
she's forbidden to lie on, that is, passionately,
and if you still want to marry me after all
these months waiting for an answer,
I can promise that life with me means
furniture will wander ceaselessly,
and I'll even goad you into chasing it

and furthermore I promise never again
to wear a ring that binds too tightly, nor
expect you to, and you can believe my fingers
are uncrossed when I say the cat, dog, child,
and house are ready, yes, all ready, yes I'll
marry you and yes and yes and yes and yes.

World Without Complaint

I. Sounds Forever Disappeared
Guns whining, barking. Rat-a-tat-tat.
Brff. Brff.
Voices grating like chalk
wrung wrong across blackboards.
Cross parents chastising children
as though coating candy in bitterweed.
Nine-tenths of the evening news.
Two-tenths of the weather report.
Currish cuss words.
Crushed-crystal silence of trust broken
when friends, spouses, kin
refuse to converse.
Loud sob of loneliness.
Sigh of lost hope.
Spit of hatred.
Churlish jangle of inequality

II. Sounds Augmented, Enhanced
Liberty bells.
Satisfied stomachs after savory meals.
Buzz of friendly discourse.
Mellow echo of courtesy.
Jingle of coins crowding
Salvation Army bucket.
Hum of a full refrigerator, warm furnace,
car full of fuel, plane traveling unguarded.
Corn popping on a snowy eve.
Parties, peace-talks, prayers, praise.
Love-making. Laughter.
Children's giggles. Christmas carols.
Multi-faith music festivals.
Applause. Angel songs
as the sun slips over the horizon
and you snug in bed, softly snoring, safe.

Two Days Before Thanksgiving

My husband got a brand new deluxe
combination grinder and mixer. For you,
he said. I've bought all my wives mixers.

I was annoyed, didn't need a mixer,
didn't want a mixer, didn't like
being lumped with all his wives.

What's that mean? I asked with an edge
but he wouldn't say. Finally: I suppose
I really bought it for myself.

The mixer—too many gadgets, heavy, tall
for the kitchen counter. I couldn't open
the cupboard doors, find a spot to store it.

I wanted a massage. I wanted him to kiss
me long, not just shallow wifely pecks.
I wanted him to court me again. I didn't

want a mixer, didn't want to feel guilty
for not appreciating him enough, to have
to hide how I felt, to disappoint him.

He grocery-shopped, fixed the turkey, made
the creamed corn, the cranberry relish. He
ground the cranberries. My daughter watched,

fascinated. I watched too, a little. I was still
disappointed but the relish looked good.
I decided. I would put the mixer

in the large cabinet by the sink
and my love for him out in the open
so he wouldn't have to guess anymore.

Love

Search the shed for the dried blocks,
the black ones dug deep, stockpiled
late in the spring.

We cut them with a sharp shovel
to make fuel for warmth, life, hope.

Set them up to dry, cure them
for another three weeks,
stack them carefully,

a labor-intensive art handed down
from generation to generation
of wise pioneers who knew

from long experience the best way
to guard against inevitable freeze.

And None of Us Young Anymore

Sis and I flew in for the service. Mother
looked good despite the daily hospital trips
and him wasting away so god-awful slowly.
No, she won't go home with either of us.
Besides, if she's going to be alone,
she might as well get used to it.

Sis and I stay up late talking.
About our marriages, our mother's marriages,
our grandmothers' marriages,
our kids' perceptions of these marriages.
About how we won't be like her, so closed.

Morning. We move plants, pictures, lamps,
the chair where he sat for months.
We find the animal shelter,
purchase an eight-week-old tabby,
tie a ribbon around his neck. Mother names
him after us, says she likes how
we moved things, seems almost happy.

Later, Sis tells how, when I was small,
Mother wouldn't talk, especially not to Dad.
I'm stunned. I'd always blamed myself
for that silent treatment. We clean the kitchen
while Mother rests in the living room,
the kitten on her lap.
Mother sits in her chair, avoids his.
Over the rattle, we hear Mother murmuring.
"Oh, what a sweet little thing you are," she purrs.

Once, after my first marriage broke,
I showed my lover a picture of Mother
as a young bride. *Something's going on
with that woman, Look at her eyes. Was she
by any chance pregnant when she married?*

I shook my head emphatically no,
said it was seven years before Sis arrived.

Now, I finally understand that my knowledge
wasn't necessarily the answer.

About Family on this Road Traveled

Family is almost the first people you tell
and when they learn you want to be a minister
they say "Go for it."
Family is who packs up cardboard
boxes, carts them in and out of U-Haul trucks
then helps unpack them.
Family rubs your back or sends you a letter
or flowers or gives you a hug when things
aren't going quite right at theological school.
Family knows what M/L, U of C, CPE, MFC mean.
Family knows what getting a "1" from the MFC means.
Family hears your first sermon six times
then tells you it was wonderful.
Family attends conferences it has only
moderate interest in, doesn't complain
when you have to go to yet one more church meeting.
Family tells you it really likes eating fast food
five nights in a row.
Family sees you with your hair messy and your face
unmasked, and knows when you just absolutely must
get some sleep.
Family spends vacation time resetting the 1-inch margins
on your doctoral thesis to 1 1/4 inches and never once
says you should have found this out sooner.
Family writes, "Good Luck, Mom" on hand-crafted paper
when you leave for your oral exam
and family plays the piano at your ordination,
does the graphics for the order of service
lights the chalice especially for you
says it doesn't mind sleeping on the couch
when the key to the guest room disappears.

For graduation, family gives you
a photo of the road traveled
to hang in your ministerial office.

Family travels miles itself to celebrate with you
whenever it can and sends love when it can't
and without family this day would never have happened
the road never traveled, no, not at all.
Thank you, Family, for being there, for being here,
for being.

My Mixed Sermon: Short, but No Jokes

It's the ill among us who need us
the needy among us who challenge us
the challengers among us who surprise us
the surprisers among us who hearten us
the heartened among us who lead us
the leaders among us who follow

the will of the ill
the pull of the needy
the demand of the challengers
the aspiration of the surprisers
the hope of the heartened.

Sister

The store was out of the picture book
I wanted to buy my sister for her 60th birthday.
The helpful clerk wrote its ISBN number.
I could check other stores, but didn't get it done.

My sister didn't make 60, the world's out of sisters
like her and it didn't even leave an ISBN number,
only memories—beautiful, rich, sometimes silly,
sometimes troubled, always caring, magnificent
images which we pass along as best we can.

Before I join my sister, I will write a book myself
just to keep those tender images alive. When I see
her next, we will share some chuckles, a few tears
over all those great pictures she made with her life
and gave away too soon.

Birthday Reunion

Everybody poses for the photograph. At first,
awkwardness. Who's in charge here anyway?
Sixty's a queen riding a float, waving, unconcerned
over details, how it all came to be. Fifty-nine finally
corrals the group on the banquet room stairs, sets

   the camera *delay* button, rushes to stand by Fourteen
   at the picture's right edge. Twenty adopts Sixty
   as a grandmother-figure needing assistance—a silly
   assumption—but Twenty, just about to marry, believes
   the world will mold to her desires. Twenty-seven,

     who recently discovered how marriage or her husband
     or both aren't all they promised, could've told Twenty
     a thing or two but in a strange unfolding of maturity,
     like a peach that ripens into sweetness slightly before
     you expect, Twenty-seven stands mute. Thirty-two sits

        on the bottom stair, holds One on her lap, wonders
        why her own infant girl is so much noisier. Forty,
        sandwiched between skinny Ten and blooming Eleven,
        eases an arm around each. At stair top Two, satisfied,
        towers from Nineteen's arms. Five, in foreground, giggles

           spontaneity like a confetti shower, wins a zillion smiles.
           Forty-seven, preparing for her first full-time settlement,
           cozies up to Sixteen. Fifty, flushed, blinks hot flashes
           on-off-on, a neon advertisement. Fifty-four, center front,
           still sore from the back surgeries (tougher than expected)

              lumbers into a folding chair. When the film's developed,
              all sixty struggle to see any real likeness to each other
              yet the wide-angle lens of this portraiture captures how
              the oldest is also the newest and how the baby's come
              faithfully to these gatherings for sixty years, always pure.

Lost Words

A daughter's gift, these words,
her mother's poetry carefully glued
to magnetic sheets, then cut apart, shuffled.
Personalized refrigerator poetry
equaled the best possible affirmation
of my hopeful poetic aspirations.

I kept some of those words on the door
for years and put the rest in covered glass.
Once, I set them all out, categorized,
like types of chocolate in an expensive box:
nouns here, verbs there. The conjunctions
formed a long line of embarrassment.

For a while, I hid the words. That was after
an editor/friend couldn't discern
enough "good" poems of mine to make
an entire book. I totally quit writing poetry,
an end like a period stuck in the middle

of a sentence. Then, when the grandchildren
learned to read, I remembered these tiny
magnetized words, wanted them
for an educational toy. Searching,
prayers to the patron saint of lost objects,
nothing brought them back.

These words included no bald realities
like orphans, denounce, abort,
nor any riches such as success, joy, completion,
enduring, potent. Still, I crave these lost words,
having discovered in their absence
how hard it is to string meaning out of each day
without being able to wire the details together
with conjunctions, prepositions, commas.

A Questionable Move

made in the December of her life
by the queer chance that her first daughter
died before she did, so sad, she says,
when she remembers,
which is less and less all the time.

Mother sits in her chair in the Home,
pushes a button to help her stand,
smiles at nameless faces, reads
the local paper but can't name
the city she lives in now.

How does one make new friends
when one is ninety and lives in a land
foreign to her mind, not the native
homestead of her childhood, the one
still alive inside her head?

Through her window, the world. Two
trees. If you ask, she'll grin, tell you
how they talk to each other. And to her,
these greening trees, her friends,
signs of the spring soon to arrive.

Chairs with Wheels

Mother got her first wheelchair shortly before
she moved here. When I phoned, her leg hurt.
She couldn't get around easily. Then, dropping
her voice almost to a whisper ... they were going
to get her a chair with wheels. She couldn't call it
a wheelchair, the concept so loaded with baggage.

Long lives make many memories. Then old age
arrives and the memory retrievers in the brain
wear out with the overload. They can only reach
the earliest memories in the pile. After a while
they lose even that mobility. The memories
need chairs with wheels. Mother's, for instance:

> Born to Maud and Will. Crawling. Cherry trees. Crib to Fern. Maud baking fruit pies. Horse-pulled postal wagon, Will leaving mail in rural mailboxes. An automobile. School. Punished for writing with the left hand. College. Teaching. Marrying Roger. Turning window shades upside down in the Great Depression. Indoor plumbing. A five-party telephone. Television. Airplanes. A baby girl. A boy. Falling, breaking an arm. Gardening. Another girl. Teaching again. A college degree. Maud (Alzheimer's) strapped into bed. Maud's funeral. Will's funeral. Teaching. Crocheting blankets for the grandkids. Teaching. Man on the moon. Roger's funeral. Moving off the farm. Learning to smoke. Marrying Cecil. Crocheting a smaller blanket: arthritis. Moving from Ohio to Texas. Wearing a hearing aid. Painting. Giving artwork to the kids, grandkids. Cecil's funeral. Moving. Fern's funeral. Moving. First girl's funeral. Chair with wheels.

oooo   oooo   oooo   oooo

When the memory-byte tower grows too tall
it topples, scatters the most recent memories
out of reach, but not gone. I grab a fistful
of my Mother's memories, stash them in photo
albums, in my writing, in my heart. I give some
away. Some lie ignored, eventually tumble off

the earth back into that collective stockpile where
all lives are fashioned. When, in the great basket
of time, they are picked out again, they form
a special intuition, a kind of partial remembering.
In her nineties, Mother still adds a few. Dinner
at my house. Great grandkids. Chairs. Wheels.

Smiling Over Her Hot Fudge Sundae

Mother announces this is likely her very last dish of ice cream.
  Are you planning on dying tonight?
  I make the question a joke, a protest.
  She expects it. I reassure her.
  What's your hurry, Mother?

It's a game we play.
Sometimes several times during one sundae.
She forgets she has already played the game.
Every time is a first time.

You mean you don't think I ought to be in any rush?
  No, don't be in any rush, Mother.
  I like having you around, Mother.

I tell her over and over, although the form varies.
Some days she still feels well enough to make this trek for the sundae.
This, the raw meaning of "happy."

When the good Lord says it's time, I'm going to say,
'Just a minute, Lord. Just let me finish this ice cream first.

Mother Laughed When She Read *"Smiling Over Her Hot Fudge Sundae"*

I really like that part about telling the Lord
to wait a moment, she says. It'd be too bad
if you don't publish it so some other women
like me can read it.

It makes me chuckle. For people my age,
it is good to chuckle. I struggle with not having
a Kleenex when I want one. Old people like me,
our noses aren't like yours. They drip more often.
I don't know why. Maybe it's the atmosphere.
My nose gets wet. I don't know why.

In ninety years I've known some strange things.
I've known some things I shouldn't know.
Don't get too curious. You might find out
something you shouldn't know. There are lots
of things in this world we shouldn't know. Don't try.

What I would like is, would you get me
some more sugar for this tea? When you get old,
you like everything sweet.

According to Mother (When Asked)

Good days are ones when I have good books to read.
Bad days are ones when I need to go to the library.

Good days are ones when I get some letters.
Bad days are ones when I don't get any mail.

Good days are ones when I go to visit my children.
Bad days are ones when I don't feel like going anywhere.

Good days are ones where I can sit in my chair, read a book.
Bad ones are ones when I need to go to the library.

Good days I wish I felt a little bit better so I could go teach school.
Good days I'd like to go to school and teach kids to read.

That's about enough.

Mother's Good vs. Bad Days, According to Me

Notes   *1=Very Bad; 10 = Excellent*

The morning before her 90th birthday party, I checked,
made sure she was dressed nicely. She'd moved cross-
country three months earlier. A hard move. On the morning
before her birthday, Mother was excited and alert,
but not feeling well. I focused on the alert part.

                              1 2 3 4 5 6 **7** 8 9 10

The afternoon before her party, I drove family,
just arrived on the airplane, to have dinner with her.
Her curtains were closed. A bad sign. She sat, disheveled,
in night gown and robe, stripped of her pretty new clothes,
ready for bed at three in the afternoon. She pulled
a blanket over her head, was nearly incoherent.

                              1 2 3 **4** 5 6 7 8 9 10

The day she turned ninety, Mother somehow managed
to make it down the hallway, through the lounge, to the room
where sixteen out-of-town relatives eagerly waited her arrival.
On the way, she told her DIL that, there for a while, she'd
thought maybe she was going to cash in her chips. Cash
in her chips? Daughter-in-law laughed, retold the story
to the others. For two hours—amidst bouquets of daffodils,
her favorite, Mother held court. Her magnificence shone.
What a trouper, everyone said. Everyone was pleased.

                              1 2 3 4 5 6 7 **8** 9 10

The day after her ninetieth birthday celebration, she went
into the hospital with pneumonia. Next few days tricky.

                              1 2 3 4 5 6 7 8 9 10

For two weeks, she was bedridden. She wore diapers.
A social worker reluctantly put Mother in extended care.
One week, she warned me. She can't stay any longer.

She needs skilled care. The social worker insisted. I
insisted back: Mother would be walking by next week.
She just needs a little longer. to regain her strength. Social
worker shook her head: May take her weeks, months.

1 2 3 4 5 6 7 8 9 10

I was wrong about how soon Mother would walk again.
She was walking *before* the middle of the next week.
The day she took a few steps with her walker—magic!

1 2 3 4 5 6 7 8 9 10

Hospital staff moved her twice in extended care. Each
time, Mother grew a little more confused, defeated.

1 2 3 4 5 6 7 8 9 10

Home again and she is a jailbird paroled, a soldier
returned, an old lady given one more chance. She
recognizes her room, her table, her love seat, her chair.
She greets family pictures, the ones hanging above
her bed that she talks to at nights. I'm home, she sings.

1 2 3 4 5 6 7 8 9 10

It is a long way from her chair to the dining room. Her
leg hurts. She's lonely. Absently, she picks at the skin-
graft on her nose, at the dressings. She pulls the bandage
off, causing us concern. I explain that she'd a cancer
removed. Right after the pneumonia. Oh, yes, she says,
folding her hands in her lap. What am I doing living here?

1 2 3 4 5 6 7 8 9 10

I buy her a box of ice cream bars, stash them in her freezer.
The refrigerator is full size, even in this small room.
Intentional, the manager explained months earlier.
The more familiar, the easier it is for these older residents.
I pull two ice cream bars free of their wrappers and we sit
next to each other like two children, enjoying.

1 2 3 4 5 6 7 8 9 10

She can't make it to the bathroom in time. Each day when
I arrive, wet pants hang in the bathroom. She's upset. Me, too,
but I tell her it's common after a senior has been hospitalized.
I say she probably just needs more time. She looks at me
the way she always has when she catches me in a lie.

1 2 3 4 5 6 7 8 9 10

They gave her a pad to help with her "problem." She grins,
says, I'm not the only one here has to wear one of these.

1 2 3 4 5 6 7 8 9 10

At the doctor's office to check out the skin graft, she waits
in her wheelchair for 1½ hours. Can we go now? she asks.
Let's just go home, she suggests. Can we go home now?
She looks at me reproachfully. A good daughter would never
let this happen. She's so uncomfortable, I swear
I will never again bring her where she has to wait so long.

01 2 3 4 5 6 7 8 9 10

We visit the grocery store, have lunch in the café,
then she waits on a bench while I quickly pile items
into a basket. She removes the pretzels, keeps the rest.
I feel like I did when I first took my kids to Disney World.
After, she's not even tired. She sits in my backyard, reads
the ice cream sundae one again, laughs out loud each time
she comes to the lines where she tells the good Lord
to wait until she finishes her ice cream. I like that part, she
says. Three times, she says it. When I ask what advice she
has for folks my age, she says people should remember their
relationships with others. Soon, she's ready to go home.

1 2 3 4 5 6 7 8 9 10

Mother's Men

Mother loves men. The other day, for instance,
I couldn't persuade her to leave her chair.
I'm too old. I don't feel well today.
I don't want to paint today. Maybe another day.

Ten minutes after I left, my husband, Dan, stopped in
and within half an hour she was sitting across from him
in a booth, eating ice cream, beaming as though she were on a date.
Dan sings to her. Old Irish songs she likes.
Then he starts a children's jingle. *To market, to market...*
    To buy a fat pig, Mother rhymes.
Home again, home again, he adds.
Jiggity jig, Mother finishes.

That's all the words Dan knows.
But Mother is not satisfied yet. She begins again.
    To market, to market, to buy a fat hog.
Dan, startled by this unfamiliar variation, turns attentive student.
    Home again, home again, jiggity jog.
Rhyme done, Mother's eyes dance.

As Her Sixty-Something Son-In-Law Leaves, Mother Says to Him

Be good.
And if you can't be good,
name it after me.

Doctor Visits

In the seven months since Mother moved here,
she's seen a dozen different doctors.

I have a runny nose, Mother says as we wait to see one
of her doctors. What do you suppose is wrong with it?

I have no clue what is wrong with Mother's nose. I study
the growing piles of used tissues which she collects

in her pockets, in her purse, in the basket on her walker.
I am tired of all these trips to see Mother's doctors.

I suppose you have a runny nose, I say, imitating
a doctor's voice. That'll be fifty dollars.

Mother studies me momentarily. Charge it, she prescribes.
Her little laugh rings the room.

Mother's Mother (In Her Words)

Monday
Who taught me to read?
My mother.
I could read even before I went to school.

Tuesday
She was quiet.

Wednesday
She was a remarkable woman.
She had a way with people.
She was always doing something for someone,
some favor, something nice.

Thursday
She was a good cook.
My favorite was fried chicken.
She let me eat it with my fingers.

Friday
Yes, she had Alzheimer's.
You wouldn't remember her the way I would.
You were too young.

Saturday
Yes, we had to put her in a nursing home.
Yes, it was hard.
But it was the *right* thing to do.

Breaking the Rules

A friend tells about caring for his mother in her last years.
Emphysema even before old age senility. That's what he
called it. *Not really Alzheimer's but the effects are the same.*
What are the effects? After I show her my poems, Mother asks:
Do I have Alzheimer's? She seems unsure, vaguely distressed.
A mistake, my being so open? The only other time I put her
and Alzheimer's together in the same sentence: denial.
I don't have Alzheimer's. Period. Suddenly I feel guilty,
wish I knew better how to care for Mother in her old-age
forgetfulness, which is what the staff here call Alzheimer's.

I feel my way along, day by day, just trying to do my best.
Sometimes I seek advice. Hence, my friend, who lugged a
sixty-pound oxygen tank in addition to a wheelchair
every time he took his mother out. I think of my own mother,
how she struggles out of her chair, walks a walker to the car,
carefully positions herself on the seat, folds her legs in one
at a time, the bad one first: *I'm sorry I'm so slow.*
I tell her we have plenty of time. I think of adding
a sixty-pound oxygen tank to this procedure. I feel lucky,

proud. It'd be so simple for Mother to quit, surely she
will use that lift chair someone upstairs is selling.
Alice-the-nurse urges: *It would be so good for her.*
What is good for Mother? Yesterday, we took the elevator
to try out the lift chair. She sat, obedient, watched as it
easily, oh so easily, helped her to her feet. She waits
until we're back in the elevator before she shakes
her head "no." When we are back in her room, she collapses
into her own chair, looks fallen. Mother, I want to say,
I was only trying to help. Mother, please don't be so sad.

Earlier, my friend tells how his mother hallucinated, how
she thought the staff was having sex on the window sills,
how she thought she was being sexually abused by an orderly
when they bathed her. Yuk! This is old age senility?

It was a painful time, my friend says. His eyes look away.
He tells me he spent maybe four hours a day with her.
I calculate, compare, feel guilty again. His regrets? Only
that she isn't still here, and also that he hadn't snuck
some wine in for her. She loved a glass of wine now and then.
If he had it to do over again, he'd break more rules.

Watson and Mother

He had a sister called Holmes.
When people ask, which they always do,
I tell them he's a cosmopolitan.
A mutt, I say, if they don't get it.
They nod. The best kind, they agree.

Mother loves Watson. She may forget
the crackers in the cupboard,
the ice cream bars in the freezer,
where she put her hearing aids,
but never the dog biscuits under the sink.
When the dog and I visit, she lights up.
Oh, you brought the dog. Her voice, the same she
uses for babies. She reaches out for his slobbery kiss.
Oh, you brought Watson. She remembers his name
better than she remembers my husband's.

Later, she accompanies us to the lobby,
the short walk not just a leave-taking,
but a pageant, every encounter en route
an opportunity to pay homage to the royal animal,
every person met recalling some dog of his or her own.
Watson greets them all, plays no favorites.

But Mother knows how to take advantage
of her social position. He's my dog, she announces
to any who would dare to doubt.
Well, actually, he's *her* dog, she adds, nodding
vaguely in my direction, a moment of conscience.
But he's my dog, too. Yes, he's *my* dog. Now *I* am
vanished, the world peopled only with Mother's dog,
Watson, and those who rightly worship him.

In dog years, Watson is nearly as old as Mother.
Once jet black except for the white bib and boots,
now he is gray around the eyes, his whiskers.

Some days he moves more slowly—arthritis
in the leg where a car once hit him. To be expected,
the vet pronounces. Also the cataracts, the loss
of hearing, of teeth. But when he sees Mother,
his tail speeds fast. He loves me, Mother says
with a certainty that I never hear her say of God.

Mother Is Right

We are sitting on the patio. Mother has just finished reading
my three latest entries. The only thing I want to say, she says,
is that I'm sorry I can't wash my own back.
      I laugh, curious how her comment relates to what she's read.

I ought to buy one of these, these … she can't find the word,
these things on a stick so I can wash my back with a stick.
      Where is the logic to this conversation?

Otherwise, I don't have any trouble washing myself.
I wash my legs, my arms, my tummy.
      Mother, I say, what made you think of washing?
      There wasn't anything in my writing about washing.

She looks puzzled, righteous. She leafs through the pages again,
then reads aloud, for my benefit:
*How she thought she was being sexually abused by one
of the orderlies when they gave her a bath against her will.
Yuk! This paranoia is old age senility?*

Mother stumbles over the pronunciation of "senility,"
      but I have clearly erred. Mother is right. There is something
      about bathing in my writing. Never underestimate Mother.
      You're right, Mother, I say, repentant.

Justified, she relaxes into a smile. I seize my chance.
      I am thinking of the piece about Watson, about the ending.
      Mother, I say, I want to ask you something. It's personal.
      What I'd like to know is, do you think God loves you?

Mother stares at me as though she can't quite follow *my* logic.
How did I jump from baths to God? Yes, she answers. Just "yes."
      I don't think I've ever heard you say that before, I say.

She gives me the look women give to their children when
they don't want any arguing. Well, she says with a laugh,
you've heard me now.

My Life Goes Back

I was born in … in … yes, that's right, in 1908.
When I first got married I wasn't very old.
How old? I can't remember. At my age now
I don't remember things as easily as I did.
A lot of things, I can't do.

I can't run around with the boys.
I used to do that sort of thing. When
I was in high school I used to run around
with a lot of them. In college, too.
That's where I met your father.
My life goes back … quite a while.
You know something? I enjoyed most of it, too.
I had good husbands.

Learning New Things

At the grocery store Mother sits in an electronic cart,
holding handlebars tight—a kid on her first roller
coaster ride. The manager explains how she pushes here
with her thumb to go forward, and here to go backward.
He starts the cart with a key, studies Mother, sets speed
at Turtle rather than Rabbit. Turtle is fast for Mother.

Mother's face wears a tightness woven of apprehension,
exhaustion, determination, and the desire to please
her daughter me. Later, she'll say she knows I'm just
trying to help. Same she knows I'm not really mean
to replace her old comfy chair, the one with the lever
on the side where she can find it, with a lift chair

that's too big and costs more than she's worth anyway.
The staff at this grocery store treat Mother as if it were
a tremendous privilege to serve her, which it probably
isn't. She needs help at the checkout counter, getting
in and out of the cart, remembering where she stashed
her walker. She needs help. Their kindness beams.

I could never do this alone, she says. She thumbs
the handlebar, traverses aisles in jerky stops and starts.
You *are* doing it alone, I pronounce, trailing alongside,
hopeful she'll be able to take the van on Thursdays,
do her own shopping. A monumental statement
of independence. Suddenly, Mother heads straight

for a stack of cracker boxes. She tenses, pushes harder
with her thumb, precisely the opposite of what she
should do to stop the cart. Too late. She crashes.
I can't do this, she repeats. I sigh. No damage done,
I say. You're doing fine, Mother. We just need
to practice more is all.

When I was little, Mother helped me over and over …
walking, talking, sewing, reading, playing the piano.

Everything. Now she is showing me how to handle
the limitations of old age. Over and over we practice.
Will I ever get it right, Mother? It's such a turtle pace,
this always learning new things.

Things I Want To Say About Being Ninety

You're old!
You're ninety!
Your children are grown!
Your children are grown and some
are almost old.
You're old!
You don't see well.
You can't hear well.
You can't write well.
You're retired.
And probably alone.

Mother Wrote It Herself

Over and over she promised she'd write something
for "our" book and then one miracle day she did.
My heart, the way her face was that day she spoke
of telling the Lord to wait before she came. Mother
says she's too ornery to die. I say she'd better not
get so ornery the Lord won't want her. We laugh.
A year ago Mother lived too far away to share
this laughter. Now I see her nearly every day. Two
days ago I brought her home for a while. She was
feeling good, watched as Dan tore out a wall to build
a bathroom on the main floor. Dan wore his working
clothes, overalls. He reminded me of my own father,
a farmer always building something. I wondered
if he reminded Mother of her father, who, at seventy,
built a new house almost single-handedly.
Mother watched Dan work. I watched her watch.
Beside her stood my grandmother, the only girl
among five siblings, watching *her* father and brothers
at work on their farm. For a long while we stood there,
my grandmother, my mother and me, watching our men,
cheering, applauding. If I could have seen far enough,
there'd have been a long line of us standing there.
Still, I don't have to see them, to hear them,
to know they are near, these bouquet bearers.
It's bouquets of love they carry. They hold them
so naturally, shelter them in such mundane wrappings,
that it's easy to miss the gift. Mother, for instance,
when she wrote about being ninety. Her handwriting
was shaky, nearly illegible. She read it to me, said
she wasn't finished, had more she wanted to say
about being ninety. I was ecstatic. It's great, Mother!
Immediately, I copied her words down, just in case
she never got around to saying more. I'm so pleased
you wrote something, I repeated, ignoring her desire
for me to wait. It'll make the book stronger, I said.
I didn't write it for the book, she voiced, almost
offhandedly. I wrote it because you asked me to.

Lamentations

Mother searches for a store where she can buy a new leg.
She wants to trade in the old one. It's a little joke.

Mother knows her leg probably won't get better,
that it could be worse, that she might not have any leg at all.

When the pain surges, though, watering her eyes, crafting dents
into her brow, it doesn't seem jokeable, dear God, surely

something exists to manage this pain. Mother spanks her leg
as though it were a naughty child. "Damn," she cries.

My own frustration expands and shrinks according to the depth
of those dents and the intensity of the damn. Mentally, I review

my options: call her doctor, say I'm sorry, call a new doctor,
insist she's just being melodramatic, say she should tolerate
the discomfort better, run away to avoid watching her suffer.

One day on the long walk to the car, her lameness lengthens
the pace and her complaints increase in frequency until they
flow over, drowning my patience. My empathy turns tail,

hides behind my fear. Oh, Mother, I don't know how else
to help! Her "Damn" haunts me, the sound
so odd and unusual coming from her cultured mouth.

Suddenly, from nowhere, a new choice!
God's grace, this choice, though well-camouflaged.

Inside the car, both of us safely buckled in, I lean over, caress
her shoulder. I'll help you with the damns, Mother, I offer.

Damn! I shout. Damn, damn, damn, damn, damn, damn!

Mother stares at me, amazed by this unprecedented effort.
At the corners of her mouth, the beginning edge of a smile.

Damn, she says.

Damn, damn, damn, damn! I echo. Loudly. I hold nothing back.
And then we laugh.

Little by Little We Slip

Dan and I stop on our way to a movie.
Mother wears her red housecoat, the old favorite
she keeps digging out of the unwashed laundry.

Two new robes hang in her closet, ignored.
She has spilled something on the blanket she uses
when she sits in her chair. She spills often these days.

Mother is happy to see us. No one is as happy to see us
as Mother is these days. She searches through items
on the table by her chair. Something is bothering her,
some problem, some question she wants to ask.

An address is what she wants. She wants to write
to my brother. She wants to be buried in Ohio.
She wants my brother to take care of it.

Already arranged, Mother, we reassure her.
He knows you want to be buried in Ohio. We all know.

I feel a little hurt. Doesn't she trust me
to take care of such an important detail?

Oh, good, Mother says. Now I can relax, Mother says.
Now I know you know.

We know, Mother.

Now I feel better, she says. Now I will sleep tonight.
I am so glad you came.

We're glad, too, Mother.

I just didn't want to put it on you, she says,
waving a shaky hand at me.

I wonder if my surprise shows. It wasn't lack of trust
at all. It was concern. Concern!

Every day I ask the Lord, 'Is this the day?'
I haven't been feeling so well lately, you know.

We know, Mother.

Dan leans over, holds her hand, sings
Oh, dear, what can the matter be? Oh, dear,
what can the matter be? Oh, dear,
what can the matter be? Johnny's so long at the fair.

Mother smiles, joins in. *Johnny's not long for the fair.*
I would join in too, but a lump slips into my throat,
a large lump that will not go away.

Just Miniscule Clots in the Arteries of Daily Living

Mother tells me she needs new books from the library
She didn't read the last batch, they weren't any good.

She's irritated because I'm late, even though I warned her.

She doesn't have anything at all to snack on,
so why didn't I take her shopping yesterday
instead of to the art museum, she was too tired
to go to the museum that day anyway.

She calls to see if I'm coming,
hangs up mid-conversation. I dial her back.
Why did you hang up on me, Mother?
Please don't hang up on me.

Oh, she says, surprised by my protest.
Once I heard your voice, I knew you were all right,
that nothing was wrong at your house, that's all.

All crossness disappears. The clots dissolve. Magic!
Vexations vanish when her refrigerator
is finally restocked and she says it's kind of fun
driving that grocery cart. Thank you for taking me.

I like taking you.

It's hard on you. I'm so slow.
I'm not worth a Tinker's Damn.

Don't say that, Mother, I command.
It's not true. Not true at all, I repeat,
and suddenly I discover a new brand of irritation:
doesn't she realize how much her presence here

means to me? How empty, this life,
without all these small frustrations
making the arteries of daily living so visible.

Einstein Missed the Point

Einstein said if you fly fast enough
through space you'll be younger
than your peers when you return.
Time is relative.

Einstein's perspective was cosmic.
It produced scholarly argument,
shock, stunned disbelief,
and the erudite discourse
of my big brother Dennis
when I was ten and impressionable

but when I was ten and impressionable
days lounged under the sun
and Christmases were planets apart
and it wasn't until I turned sixty-five

yesterday that I figured out how
to tell the truth about tomorrow.

On Being a Woman of a Certain Age

Perhaps you aren't such a woman yet. Perhaps
you are not even a woman and will never experience
being of a certain age. I've known men who are distinguished,
men who are gems, men who have aged with refinement, gentility,
kindness, generosity, humility, and the wisdom not to endlessly repeat
the same worn jokes. I've known several old goats, but not one single
man of a certain age. Being of a certain age is a bit like giving birth—
you have to be female to do it. Yet it is not giving birth. No
woman of a certain age gives birth, at least not in any
traditional sense.

I am a woman of a certain age. I speak with authority, authenticity.
Contrary to popular conception, to be a woman of a certain age
has nothing to do with brittle nails or frizzled hair or wires
in bra cups, although being a woman of a certain age
may include removing such wires. It may even
involve wearing high necklines, but
that is habit hangover rather than character trait.
Being a woman of a certain age has more subtle signs.
This subtlety yields mystery, not confusion. When you spot
a woman of a certain age walking into a room, you recognize her
               immediately, effortlessly

even while you can't tell why. You may
suspect it's the confidence of her walk
or the ease of her greeting or the sense
radiating from her that she understands
the pattern of the universe, how it all fits
together. The truth is that being a woman

of a certain age
requires specialized skills. The rule is, it's a closed society,
the elect, the chosen ones. If you don't know, you don't know.
You will need either to wait until you become such a woman
to discover how to be one, or (apologies if this sounds tough)
be ignorant.

At the Front Window

The bare trees open the view.
Far away on the hill, miniature cars
form a tiny train, lit up and moving fast

into the winter of my years
where their sound grows weak
and mostly stays inside

like a companion hired to sit,
plus I can't find the name of that noise
a train makes anymore either

yet I have faith that the next round
of green leaves will bring it back
in only a few more moments.

I'll open the window and though I know
there are really only cars
up there in my vista,

I'll think of summers long ago,
when the trains lived nearby
and marked time clear as a cuckoo

with their toot-toot call.

Have You Reached the Part about the Lightning?[2]

He wanted to know, thought I'd like it. Eager,
I turned pages, days. My faith, a devoted dog.

Suffering, dope lords, the cop and the psychologist
in love, the doubters, murders, fears, the black Cuban

and his mother whom everyone liked. I read
in snatches, whenever—the cat sitting on my lap,

at the bookstore over mocha, visiting the grandkids,
couched in my library my back hurting again.

Words bathed me. I luxuriated in their bubbles,
kept turning pages, maybe the lightening would be

next, tomorrow. Lightning. Lightening lightning.
The pages burst with conundrums: God and

belief, the Shiny One and Christians, gold Twinkies
thrown down from heaven both bad and good.

From what he'd said I knew I wouldn't find the part
about the lightning until maybe the middle

but I passed the halfway mark one noon waiting
in the jeep for him to finish an errand at Lowes.

Old now, I read like a beggar and still no lightning.
But the snow blowing tonight, a blizzard advisory—

another thing altogether, and us snug inside
raiding the refrigerator for leftover turkey, satisfied.

---

[2]With appreciation to Michael Gruber for his *Valley of Bones*

My Husband the Genius

Almost an octogenerian, he is still
teacher, electrician, plumber, builder,
chemist, cook, professional showman,
wood carver, humorist, theorist, problem

solver, caring brother, dedicated father,
loving spouse and my best friend,
but I'd forgotten the genius part
until I found

on the back of an essay
I'd labored over far too long
and had printed out for yet more study
on the blank side of discarded

scratch paper he'd given me
back when we lived amidst younger
walls, passions, insights
the grabbing voice of his old poems

> Song of My First House
> The Cat, the Lady and the Artist
> Something Is Going On
> Unclean

the fourth of which spoke of dirt
in the crack of his fingers
as he cleaned a sewer at midnight,
how the water freezing around his feet

was honest and clean, cleaner
than the paper he wrote on
and instantly I was swept
back into wonder, thrill, expectation

and the irresistible urge to answer
his mesmerizing meter.

The Christmas We Bought Each Other Hearing Aids

our live tree cost a small fortune.
It felt sinful spending so much
on an artifact so soon doomed.

These days our own tree of life
drops people, friends, like needles
several to cancer, one to the liver
(too much hard drinking long ago)
another to mean genes, her children
still thinking they'll escape.

My spouse and I hang on by sheer will,
ignoring all degenerative processes
which, even as we breathe, eat
the vitality under our skin.
When he sleeps he snores loudly
but I never wear those aids at night.
There are certain advantages...

Besides, no one needs them at all
to hear the angels sing. When they
finally cart the bared tree
to the recycling park, a celestial song
soothes the way. Lullaby.

When I Am Alone

I read aloud, an exercise they say will
help me process words. I scored 50%
on the word-processing part of my last
hearing test. I misheard half the words,
an embarrassingly low score: shame!

My latest hearing aids have five
programs. One for gatherings. One for TV.
One for movies or plays or listening
to sermons at churches equipped
with certain special hearing systems.
One for 360° car conversations.
One for normal talks,
none of which are really normal.

When I am alone I can forget I might
lose my job because I guess at what
they are saying and I pretend I understand
when I don't, and I get tired of straining
to distinguish between speak and week,
hope and cope and joke, learning
and yearning. It's surprising
what rhyme does not do to inform
a conversation. I often repeat

whatever I heard up to the part I misheard:
I make my voice end with a question
mark. I want my conversation partner
to repeat only the missing word instead
of everything previous, but it seldom works
that way. Simply put, I need to see it to hear it.
Like on my Caption Phone, a marvelous
invention provided to me absolutely free
through taxes we all pay for the Disabilities Act.

I am grateful for all the new technology.
I do my best. But when I am alone
I don't have to do my best, a welcome rest.

Sabbathing

Today my skeleton steps out from my skin,
walks through snow tall as my ribs, holds
my head high. My heart blankets my liver,
eyes peek beneath a scalp full of gray,
mottled skin puddles the floor like eggs
cracked open.

It's a wake-up call to lose structure
this way. I lie by the window, wonder what
I'll turn into when it returns, climbs in,
makes me watch the clock again, go here,
do this, that.

Renewal used to be so easy, but now
it takes longer, requires commitment.
Even the Divine needs hands, though,
to bake a cake.

Holy, Holy, Holy

this day when Coalition forces finally kill
a long-sought enemy in the Middle East,
when the President arrives/departs our city
with no unseemly incident, leaves behind
relieved lawmen, limp observations
about immigrants, border control, America,
when the perpetrators of four separate
but ghastly murders this year remain free
and yesterday's news, and the morning paper
front-pages a downtown tax, school districts
which continue to sport Indian mascots,
causing state educators consternation

this day when one woman, a thousand miles
east, heads for work wondering how much
longer her cancer-ridden husband will last, when
Mr. & Mrs. Long-Married check airline schedules
so they can fly a thousand miles west to visit
their grown son living (barely) with congestive
heart disease, when two people who don't
even know each other take the same anti
depressants prescribed by the same doctor,
and John Doe (sober, suicidal, celebrating
his 61st birthday) wonders if he can make it
another year until social security kicks in

this day when the geranium cuts wintered
indoors are rooting, budding in the back yard,
when the old neighbor man, repairs complete,
wheels a small bicycle down the street
for the little neighbor girl to ride, when, two states
away, the four grandchildren climb into car seats
(the law requiring ever more precautions)
and my daughter loads a picnic in the back,
drives to the pool, when I, just off the phone
with her, trim the roses my spouse gave me after
Monday's surgery, check my newly-biopsied
breast, note the bleeding has actually stopped

The Weed that Turned into a Zinnia

In the spring, at the new house
along a row of established peonies
I planted cosmos, zinnias, poppy seeds,
nasturtiums. When summer arrived

I saw I'd planted them too close
to those seasoned old perennials. Not
enough light everything needed every
thing was hard I was tired, worked best
I could, but my faith … a lost sun.

A few flowers appeared anyway
in the pretense of a row. Cosmos?
I transplanted them where there
was more light. I watered them,
loved them as they grew. And grew.

But no flowers. My spouse wondered
why I'd planted weeds in pots.
After the stalks grew stiff and huge,
I got rid of them, plucked God right out
of the dirt, tossed away all sense of sacred.

I argued with my spouse, finally admitted
wrong, pitched those blasted weeds
in the yard waste. Then in the sheen
of early autumn I spotted a lone zinnia
blooming under the withering peonies.

Weathered, I left it alone, took only
the joy of survival, which I stuck deep
in my heart, hoping.

Wave At Each Other

My friend the hoarder collected books, kept them
all over his house on shelves lined like library stacks.
After he died his needy wife and unmarried daughter,
the one who stayed, made a little trail from the front
door to the refrigerator. Inside, piles of Chinese take-out

in white Styrofoam, one on top of another on top
of another. When the wife died too, the daughter, crazy
but kind, sold the house "as is," moved to an apartment.
That was twelve years ago and although I lost track,
I never stopped wondering whether her new home

is one more labyrinth. I stuck that wonder in my head
where it's remarkably simple to retrieve even though
it's smothered by other curiosities: what makes lonely
people lonely, why the cousin I played with as a kid
never talks to me anymore, how my son is coping

with his job transition, why my spouse, without whom
I'd be bereft, said almost nothing about me in his memoirs
while I pasted him all over the pages of mine, why I just
wave at a person I'd really like to know better, why
he waves back, why shadow space is sometimes best, oh

my head is so full from years of stockpiling, stashing,
accumulating, squirreling away, hiding, secreting,
and otherwise storing wonders of my life for future use
that I fear I won't even be able to find my way to my arm
anymore, let alone lift it high.

Memory Pill

I took my first memory-enhancing
pill today. Two doc appointments
ago and a whole morning of tests
        "say these numbers backwards"
        "here's a list of items, name
        the furniture" …

the diagnosis was mild cognitive
impairment. I've had it ten years,
maybe longer. It's contagious
—spouse, friends. It's called

"failing some," as when I told
my daughter that my spouse was
failing some. Always remember
to add the "some."

My daughter called this morning.
While we were talking, I walked
around the house, searching hard.
Upstairs. Downstairs. In the kitchen.
My phone was missing from my pocket.

I was frustrated. "I can't find
my cell phone," I complained.
"Aren't you holding it?" she asked.

Should've taken the whole bottle!

Sometimes, When the Flowers Need Watering

I don't want to. One small,
negative thought next to all
the others cluttering the mind
with ceaseless frenzy.

A sense of humor is a wonderful
thing in a woman, my spouse observes.
My spouse cooks, brings roses,
vacuums, puts freshly laundered sheets
back on the bed, mows the lawn
but seldom waters the flowers,
can't see their desperation.

It's nothing we ever talk about,
this insatiable, repetitive, endless,
boring need of the poor, wilting
plants to be nurtured alive, green.

Untitled

Old man futility is hovering
over my shoulder again. My third eye
catches him fiddling with my inner ear.

As always he looks strong, invincible
but hides his face. *Let me in*, he pleads.
It'll feel familiar, comfortable.

My mother housed him most of her life.
Then he discovered me and I lugged him
around for years as if I had no choice.

One day I found my daughter holding him
tightly, like a lover. I watched, weeping,
while he tried to wreck her self-esteem,

mangle her mind. An old soul though, she
prevailed. I call her to let her know
he's back. I share what he's whispering.

She's quicker than I, this daughter. *Tell him
he's lying, Mother. Familiar maybe, but
comfortable? Tell him he's lying, Mom.*

My voice gains power as I practice. *Liar*,
I yell. *Liar. Liar.* I spit on his feet, a first
for me, and he slinks off, skunked.

Sisters-by-Law

We'd expected to take her
out to lunch, but when we arrived
she just wasn't up to it.
We visited for a while
then said our goodbyes
not knowing they would be so final.

It's always like that, even
when we know better. God
made us so we just don't want
to let go

of the phone calls, the cards
for all the holidays even Saint
Paddy's Day, the sunshiny garage
sale-ing, the hand-crocheted
table toppers, the cross-country
trip, the confidences shared,
even that hard hospital visit
a while back when things
weren't looking too good
though the prayers still seemed
to work

But maybe our prayers now
will work too, the ones
that free her from tag-along
turmoil, that request perfect peace
and God's eternal embrace
and love that never ever never
stops, only just keeps expanding

the way her kindness always did.

On the Eve of a Hard Seventy

I woke with the vision of turning blue,
not some septic faded holey denim,
the kind I wore as a teen and lived long
enough to watch the style disappear,
then return recently to racks of clothes
in quality stores with senseless price tags

nor the pale sky-blue of a bright summer
day, just the way it was on the late August
date when I turned seventy, a blue
that shouted light-hearted joy completely
foreign to the actual event

which started out with an email
from my old high school buddy Mary, the one
who moved to Mexico when she married
and four decades later we reconnected
via cyberspace and she wished me
*a memorable 70th birthday and that the coming
year brings you only success and joy*

and then confided that her beloved cancer-
wracked spouse had finally succumbed
Saturday morning. She added a long missive
detailing the scene, how they declined
(at his request) a religious service, then had one
anyway, the family—all dressed in Yucatan beige
and white (a guayabera) gathering around him—
sharing memories and tears, how *they'd left
the coffin open so everyone could say
a last good bye, except for one grandson who
just couldn't bear the idea of seeing his "Abu"
gone*, no it wasn't that kind of sky-blue at all

but rather, my skin was turning *cobalt*,
becoming that startling, rich, unignorable blue

that often crams the pages of today's most
sophisticated decorator magazines, skin so
shocking that it stuck out, demanding attention,
not denial, and after that it didn't bother
me to be turning seventy since this new
brilliant blue somehow made me beautiful.

Bouncing Boxes

Today in the fifth season of our lives
my spouse tells about the shards of china
spilt from a cardboard box bouncing
off a truck and dancing down the highway
before him into a census of ever smaller
pieces. I love his images, love him, but
for a moment I hate those boxes those
bouncing boxes filled with the clutter
of our past and threatening to smack us
through the windshield of our faces, cut
the thin skin around our hearts, bruise.

Today I sit, reread his poem, remember
years ago when my in-laws, my tiny
daughter and a very pregnant me were
en route from Cincinnati to Flagstaff,
eager for Rt 66 and other kicks in a new
home, new start, the next episode in what
I now think of as the second season
of my life. My then-spouse was finishing
a thesis while we four found us a home.
The minimal necessities of living—
card table, folding chairs, sheets, dishes,
clothes—were crammed into a makeshift
box tied to the top of our beat-up car,
just like Okies, when suddenly it burst,
scared the residents of cars behind us but
(small past miracle) chairs, clothes, china,
card table … everything missed them all.

Today I sit in my chair, think of boxes
bouncing off trucks, re-imagine them
as boxes filled with wishes come true
flying fast in every direction, spreading.

The Seasons of our Emotions

There are times in our lives
when the creek runs dry,
when no poetry flows,
when the children aren't tucked
safely in bed, when our love
is wrung out in emptied bed pans,
wheelchairs, the job that didn't
work out, when inside our human
skins is only air and science,
and outside even the train
wails in the middle of the night.

Then there are times in our lives
when the river rises dangerously high,
when love, pain, hope, disappointment,
anxiety, trust all crowd together
against the thin shores of our beings,
when a whole year goes by in one week,
when we fear the family tree
might be uprooted and even the church
swept away, when the waters make wild,
raucous music, when it's hard
to build up the banks fast enough.

There are times of ice,
when all is frozen,
and times when the colored leaves
of our lives fall gently into the stream,
forming a rainbow on land.
Yet somehow, between wax and wane,
cold and colored,
the water waves on, bearing all,
nurturing … cleansing …
and when we watch from high windows,
the stunning depth of its beauty
awakens our faith.

In My Garden

This month: the anniversary
of my only brother's birth.
Eighty-one, I think.
I emailed, then called.
No response.
I forgot to re-call.
I hope he's okay.

In my garden,
the metaphors are wilting.
I pray for rain and suddenly
I want to remind my brother
of that time long ago
when I got stuck on the log
fallen over the creek,
was too scared to move.

Brother came back for me,
held out his hand,
helped me across.

Waiting for the Number

4 I am standing on painted steel, my father's
legs gripping my trunk, his hands like vises
on my arms. I flap, a bird caged. Ahead, backs
of familiar heads appear, disappear, reappear
like a wiper sweeping rain off a windshield.
But today, only sun at Euclid Park. Metallic lattice
swings, straightens, and the ground is near, then far,
then near. My older siblings' thrilled screams
float close in the air but the sound pouring
from my mouth is pure fear. Later, when my tiny foot
finally touches ground again, my father's face
is stricken and his voice shakes. *She's too young
for roller coasters, too young, it was all I could do
to hold on to her, to keep her from jumping off.*

10 I am driving the tractor, the tractor attached
to the baler, the baler attached to a wagon,
the wagon loaded with hay and I am driving
around a corner, around a corner too fast
and the field of newly raked hay rises sideways,
nearly parallel to the tractor-baler-wagon line.
In the same long instant, an instant so long
it holds a whole line of life, the hayfield decides
to lie back down again, again I am driving
the tractor, the tractor attached to the baler,
the baler attached to a wagon, the wagon
loaded with hay, only now I am older, changed.

13 I am hanging midair while my feet wait
ground, never quite finding it, yet each time close,
the ocean comes with it, covers my head,
turns the world into water. Water fills spaces
like flood fills wood. I am water-logged. I am filled.
I sink. My mind slips into reverse, my life flashes
through it fast, a movie reel spun out of control,
so tiring, I'm tired, water slaps my arms, mouth, nose,
eyes. Hard it slaps. I push it away, push something,

someone away, I shove, shove, shove, so worn, so used
by water filling me so full, where did the air go?
so sad, sad, sad, I'm so young. Suddenly, inexplicably
strong hands tie tired arms to my tired sides, the water
yields and I lie on new ground, gasping, grateful.

18 I am sitting in the white car, my father's white
car, the car I borrowed to visit my boyfriend,
the white car stilled in an intersection
on a rural road somewhere close to a white house,
my boyfriend's house, my boyfriend's white farm
house close to the white car yet too far away
for my boyfriend to see, for anyone to see, how my hands
steer the wheel of the white car pointed south
while the gray car points east and a man with the look
of startled deer stares from the driver's seat of the gray
car crunching my father's white car right by my left
arm where steel crumbles, the wheel pinches
my stomach, the window kisses my forehead,
kiss of death? But, no. Instead I crawl over the seat,
exit the passenger door, unharmed.

30 I am perching, impotent, in the passenger seat
of a single-engine Cessna. My husband-
the-new-pilot is busy. Behind us our children
scream. Their hands mute their popping ears.
We spin tight circles in air while the ground
flies closer to us, caught by the strong magnet
of a mistake, of trying to break through
a cloud layer too thick to hold a hole wide open.
The new-pilot-my-husband struggles to control
the plane, a spinning top in dense clouds. Earth
rises up to hold us forever and ever amen, six
seconds left, five, four, then a blessed miracle, earth
retreats, the magnet dies but we, incredibly, don't.

57 I lie between white sheets, plastic ribbons
streaming from my arms, a pink cloud of pain
covering the room like a tent with no provision

for escape. I gaze at a haze of nurses, doctors,
visitors. The first surgery failed. I concentrate
on the promise of a second one. I stare, glare
at the promise, but pink pain occludes it.
Pink pain grows like smoke on a huge fire.
It singes my heart, this pain pinking around me
like a silent swindler stealing hope, the will
to live. I am thin, thinner than I was only weeks
ago. Everything about me is thin—my hands,
my trust, my patience, all my virtues, every
thing except the pink pain, which threatens
to congeal into a hard braid of self-pity, despair,
defeat. I finger the flower button connected
to the morphine ribbon, push it gently, wait
for a dust of relief to wash the flesh clean.

62 Asphalt flows beneath my car. The rug of life
(still green on the edges and rich with the harvest)
rolls under wheels as the car treads the changing season.
Today, autumn's colors peak through my windshield,
waft me with nostalgia, freshen the air with joy.
How much longer, I wonder, 'til my number's finally up?
Then I realize that when we peer at the hands
on the meaning clock, it's all heroic pulse.

74 I am social distancing these past three months
seems like years. My daughter suggested
I collect my poems into a history of my life, has been
helping with this task, sketching possible covers,
planning the layout, doesn't want these storied poems
to disappear
                                                                  when I do ...
She travels 200 miles to spend six hours with me,
flaunts pandemic guidelines when she offers a timid hug.
This morning she'd told her kids how *her* mommy
was baking pork chops and apples just for her today,
a real treat she says, though I gather they couldn't
quite see why. No matter. Their treats will be different
in fifty years, but the satisfied contentment
that seasons my soul just now will stay.

We Were Going to Have a Party

to celebrate my 75th birthday. My children
were planning it, making arrangements,
an invitation list. Then coronavirus crushed
party plans. There'd have been cake. Flowers,
a huge vase, likely zinnias from my garden
since those were the only seeds I'd harvested
last season and now I avoid stores, haven't
mastered phone delivery, other challenges.
Still, I'm zoom-fluent now, will even preach
soon at Zoom Church, how we always adapt
during these curious, uncertain, changing days.

Earlier this month I found two 4-leaf clovers
in a garden space the size of two hardcover
dictionaries, what are the odds of that? I gave
one to Dan for extra luck, which he needs
right now and mailed my son-in-law the other
in a yellowed birthday card from my dwindling
stock. He was pleased. The house Dan bought
pre-pandemic with a plan to flip it (did I say
Dan is 83?) is nearly ready and what a project!
Me on my knees, painting, on a ladder painting,
hours and hours of sweat equity. Dan working
inside walls, installing showers, toilets, sinks,
and me making sandwiches most days, the two
of us like newlyweds, often lunching on the re-
furbished porch, both still healthy and safe,
wanting to make this fifth season of our years
full of new ways to manifest our love.

Then, surprise! We had the party that wasn't
a party, the kids ordering a huge *carding*
on our front lawn. Friends drove by, honked.
Family zoomed. A glorious pot of green plants
graced a portable table under the huge pine
by the drive. Needles, sap—everything blessed.

Acknowledgements

Prologue

"The World Keeps Shifting" was published in the *Writers' Journal*, January/February 2009, p11.

A Short History of Grandmothering

Earlier versions of "May Day" and "Old Fashioned Treasure Hunt" appeared in *Possum, Beaver, Lion: Variants*, by Sarah Voss, Finishing Line Press, 2017, p35 and p4.

"Thirteen" and "Sixty-nine" received honorable mention in the Poetry Across the Generations Contest, Sigma Phi Omega, Omaha, UNO, 2014, and were also included in *Possum, Beaver, Lion: Variants*, by Sarah Voss, Finishing Line Press, 2017, p8 and p9.

"Taking Grandson to His Piano Lesson" was a finalist for the 2019 Princemere Poetry Prize.

"Fifteen" appeared in *Chalice Connection*, a quarterly publication of the First Unitarian Church of Omaha, July 2020.

"Requests" was published online in *Fellowship of Prayer*, January, 2009.

"Hard Decisions" was published in the poetry centerfold of *Elderberries*, a quarterly publication of the Unitarian Universalist Retired Ministers and Partners Association (37:2) www.UURMaPa.org Spring 2021, p9.

Like a Polaroid Picture Developing While I Watched

"Perfume" was published in *The American Muse: A Treasury of Lyric Poetry*, Knoxville, TN: Fine Arts Press, 1984, p198.

"Just Once in My Life" appeared in *Lucky Star*, (2:3) Oak Park: IL Erie Street Press, 1985, p21.

"Going to Mother's on Her Eightieth Birthday" was published as the "Metro Muse" of Omaha's weekly newspaper *Metropolitan: Omaha's News, Opinions, & Entertainment Weekly,* ca 1988.

"Reflections on Doing Nothing" was published in *Zero: Reflections about Nothing* by Sarah Voss (Notre Dame, Indiana: Cross Cultural Publications, Inc.), 1996, pp4-5.

"Blessings from the Bride's Mother" appeared in *Voice to Voice, Heart to Heart* by Sarah Voss (Boston: Skinner House) 1996, pp65-6.

"Portrait by an Unknown Girl" was published in *Earth's Daughters* (68) 2006, p41, and in *Thema* (18:2) Summer, 2006, p92.

The Past Revisited Is a Door Ajar

An earlier version of "After" appeared in *Ellipsis* (43) 2007, p5.

"The Gravel Road" was an invited poem, published in *Omaha Magazine,* November. December 2018, p51.

Nine of the poems included in this section were part of a hand-crafted-calendar I made as gifts for family for the year 1989, having visited my hometown of Austinburg, Ohio and the surrounding area during 1988 on the occasion of my 25th Geneva High School reunion.

To Ride the Wheels of Change Sweetly

"Old Full Baskets" Published in *The Nebraska English Counselor* (32:3) Spring, 1987, p33.

"Forty" appeared in *Broomstick,* (8:6) Nov/Dec 1986, p21.

An earlier version of "The Church, the Stone, and the Grass Widow" was published in *The Nebraska English Journal* (34:4), Summer 1989, pp69-70.

"Songs of Tomorrow" was published in *The Nebraska English Journal,* Fall/Winter, 1990.

"Violets" appeared in *Whole Notes* (5:1) 1989, p14.

"Exactly" was in *The Porcelain Toad*, Spring 1988, pp19-20.

"Second Chance" was scheduled to appear in the "Metro Muse" section of the *Metropolitan* the week after the weekly Omaha newspaper went out of business (ca 1990).

"Love" was published in *The Mid-America Poetry Review,* The Mid-America Press 7:3, Winter, 2006-07, p176.

Conversations with My Ninety-Year-Old Mother

"Smiling Over Her Hot Fudge Sundae," "Mother's Good vs. Bad Days (According to Me)," and portions of several other poems in this collection appeared with different titles and slightly different forms in *Soul Stories: Living with Alzheimer's*, reflections on "Sharing Ways of Caring" by Sarah Voss (in the Chapter Newsletter of the Cleveland Area Alzheimer's Association. September, 2001). My mother, Dorothy Henderson Jones, died in February, 2001, one month short of turning 93. She was buried in Chagrin Falls, Ohio, next to her first husband, Roger Henderson and her oldest daughter, Mary Lynn Nichols.

Fifth Seasoner

"The Christmas We Bought Each Other Hearing Aids" and "On Being a Woman of a Certain Age," appeared in *Celebrate: Vol. IX* (PWSA, University of Nebraska at Omaha, March, 2005, pp64 and 65.

"Have You Reached the Part about the Lightning?" and "Holy, Holy, Holy" both appeared in *Nebraska Presence: An Anthology of Poetry* (Omaha: The Backwaters Press) 2007, pp152-3.

"When I Am Alone" was the featured poem at a workshop on "Deaf Culture Awareness in a Medical Setting" presented to employees of the Nebraska Methodist Hospital in Fall, 2018.

"Untitled" appeared online in r.kv.ry *Quarterly Literary Journal,* July, 2011. An interview with the author about the poem can be found at http://rkvryquarterly.com/interview-with-sarah-voss/.

"On the Eve of a Hard Seventy" and an earlier version of "The Weed that Turned into a Zinnia" were first published in *Possum, Beaver, Lion: Variants* by Sarah Voss, Finishing Line Press, 2017, pp28-9 and p10.

"The Seasons of Our Emotions" was included in *Voice to Voice: Heart to Heart,* by Sarah Voss (Boston: Skinner House) 1996, pp41-3.

"From Waiting for the Number," a selection from the larger poem which appears in this volume, appeared in *The Midwest Quarterly,* Pittsburg State University, (52:4) p414, Summer 2011.

About the Author

Sarah Voss is the author of two chapbooks of poetry, one a book of poem prayers written in 1991 when she was transitioning from a career as a math teacher to one as minister, and the other from Finishing Line Press written in 2017 after she retired from ministry. She's published extensively on religion and math/science and is an experienced Grandmother.

More Praise
for *Poems from the Gravel Road*

In this charming collection of poems, Sarah Voss captures the persistence of memory and joy and heartache growing old in this brave new world of technology.
 —**Ruth Glick**, prolific, award-winning and best-selling author of romance, mystery, suspense, young adult and children's books, healthy cookbooks, and dozens of romance novels, many of the latter under the pen name Rebecca York.

In *Poems from the Gravel Road*, Sarah Voss offers works which move from the crafty innocence of childhood to the maturity of marriage, motherhood, and aging. The poems range from sestina to free verse and from engaging amusement to tender sadness. She tells the reader that her "new flowers always overflow / my cup with reliability and surprise," and the people in her poems overflow in the same way. She traces the passage of time, love, and life with sensitivity, especially in the complex tensions of affection and frustration in dealing with an aging parent. These poems display determined courage and strength when facing disappointment and delight–with traces of melancholy, but no despair or self-pity. What more can we ask of poetry?
 —**Michael Skau**, emeritus Professor, Department of English at the University of Nebraska at Omaha. Skau was the 2013 winner of the William Kloefkorn Award for Excellence in Poetry. His poetry publications include *Me & God* (Wayne State College Press, 2014) and chapbooks *After the Bomb* (2017) and *Old Poets* (2018), both published by WordTech Editions. He is founder and host of the Imaginary Gardens Reading Series.

www.ingramcontent.com/pod-product-compliance
Lightning Source LLC
Chambersburg PA
CBHW020233170426
43201CB00007B/408